THE
MARRIAGE
TOPICAL BIBLE

KING JAMES VERSION

PNEUMALIFE PUBLISHING

Pneuma Life Publishing books are available at discounted prices for bulk purchase for fund-raising, premiums, sales promotions.

For details, email your request to **sales@pneumalife.com** or write us at **Pneuma Life Publishing, 12138 Central Ave, Suite 251, Mitchellville, MD 20721**

THE MARRIAGE TOPICAL BIBLE
Published by Pneuma Life Publishing
12138 Central Ave, Suite 251,
Mitchellville, MD 20721
www.pneumalife.com

JUNE 2025

All rights reserved. No part of this publication may be reproduced, distributed, or transmitted in any form or by any means, including photocopying, recording, or other electronic or mechanical methods, without the prior written permission of the publisher, except in the case of brief quotations embodied in critical reviews and certain other non-commercial uses permitted by copyright law. For permission requests, write to the publisher, addressed "Attention: Permissions Coordinator," at the address below.

Unless otherwise noted, all Scriptures quotations are from the KJV of the Bible

Copyright © 2025 by D. Stewart
All Rights Reserved
Printed in the United States of America
ISBN 978-1-56229-874-6

Table of Contents
THE MARRIAGE TOPICAL BIBLE
FOUNDATIONAL MARRIAGE TOPICS

God's Design for Marriage	2
The Purpose of Marriage	3
Marriage as a Covenant	4
One Flesh Unity	4
Marriage Reflecting Christ and the Church	5
God's Heart for Marriage	6
Marriage Before the Fall	7
The Sacred Nature of Marriage	8
Marriage as God's First Institution	8
Divine Blessing on Marriage	9
Marriage and God's Glory	10
The Eternal Perspective of Marriage	11
Marriage as Partnership	11
Choosing a Godly Spouse	12
Preparing for Marriage	13
The Wedding Covenant	14
Leaving and Cleaving	15
Establishing a Christian Home	16
Marriage and God's Will	16
The Sanctity of the Marriage Bed	17

Marriage and Holiness	18
Growing Together Spiritually	19
Marriage and God's Faithfulness	19
The Beauty of Marriage	20
Marriage and Divine Love	21
God's Protection Over Marriage	22
Marriage as Ministry	22
The Joy of Marriage	23
Marriage and God's Presence	24
Honoring Marriage	25

ROLES AND RESPONSIBILITIES

Biblical Roles in Marriage	28
Loving Your Wife as Christ Loved the Church	29
The Husband as Head	29
Servant Leadership in Marriage	30
The Wife as Helper	31
Submission in Marriage	32
Mutual Submission	32
Honoring Your Husband	33
Respecting Your Spouse	34
Protecting Your Marriage	35

Providing for Your Family	35
Nurturing in Marriage	36
Leading Your Family Spiritually	37
Supporting Your Spouse's Dreams	37
Being a Godly Example	38
Responsibility and Accountability	39
Stewardship in Marriage	39
Being Your Spouse's Best Friend	40
Encouraging Your Partner	41
Building Up Your Spouse	42

LOVE AND INTIMACY

Unconditional Love in Marriage	44
Expressing Love Daily	44
Love Languages in Marriage	45
Romantic Love	46
Intimate Communication	47
Physical Intimacy in Marriage	47
Emotional Intimacy	48
Spiritual Intimacy	49
Growing in Love	50
Sacrificial Love	50

Passionate Love	51
Tender Affection	52
Demonstrating Love	52
Love Through Actions	53
Speaking Words of Love	54
Love in Difficult Times	54
Rekindling Romance	55
Celebrating Your Spouse	56
Intimate Friendship	57
The Song of Solomon Marriage	58

COMMUNICATION

Godly Communication in Marriage	60
Speaking Truth in Love	61
Listening with Understanding	61
Healing Words	62
Avoiding Harmful Speech	62
Conflict Resolution	63
Arguing Righteously	64
Gentle Responses	64
Encouraging Words	65
Speaking Blessings	66

Communication During Crisis	66
Vulnerable Sharing	67
Active Listening	68
Nonverbal Communication	68
Restoring Communication	69

FORGIVENESS AND HEALING

Forgiveness in Marriage	72
Seeking Forgiveness	72
Forgiving Deep Hurts	73
Letting Go of the Past	74
Healing from Betrayal	75
Restoring Trust	75
Overcoming Offense	76
Grace in Marriage	77
Mercy in Relationships	78
Second Chances	78
Healing Broken Hearts	79
Restoration After Failure	80
Covering Each Other's Weaknesses	80
Moving Forward Together	81
Redemption in Marriage	82

MARRIAGE CHALLENGES

Overcoming Marriage Problems	84
Surviving Difficult Seasons	84
Financial Stress in Marriage	85
Dealing with In-Laws	86
Infertility and Marriage	86
Parenting Challenges	87
Career and Marriage Balance	88
Health Issues in Marriage	88
Depression and Marriage	89
Addiction Recovery in Marriage	90
Rebuilding After Affair	90
Pornography and Marriage	91
Anger Management	92
Jealousy and Insecurity	92
Growing Apart	93
Mid-Life Marriage Crisis	94
Empty Nest Season	95
Aging Together	95
Loss and Grief in Marriage	96
Spiritual Differences	97
Cultural Differences	98

Blended Family Challenges	98
Military Marriage	99
Long-Distance Marriage	100
Childless by Choice	101

SPIRITUAL LIFE TOGETHER

Praying Together	104
Studying God's Word Together	105
Worshiping as a Couple	105
Serving God Together	106
Spiritual Growth in Marriage	107
Accountability in Marriage	107
Fasting Together	108
Ministry as a Couple	109
Evangelism in Marriage	110
Discipleship in Marriage	110
Church Life and Marriage	111
Giving as a Couple	112
Spiritual Warfare in Marriage	113
Seeking God's Will Together	114
Building a Legacy	114

PRACTICAL MARRIAGE LIFE

Daily Rhythms in Marriage	118
Creating Traditions	118
Celebrating Milestones	119
Date Night Importance	120
Vacation and Rest	121
Hospitality in Marriage	121
Managing Household Duties	122
Financial Partnership	123
Decision Making Together	123
Goal Setting as a Couple	124
Time Management	125
Building Friendships as a Couple	125
Social Life in Marriage	126
Technology and Marriage	127
Work-Life Balance	127
Retirement Planning	128
Health and Wellness Together	129
Recreation and Fun	130
Learning Together	130
Supporting Each Other's Growth	131
Creating a Peaceful Home	132

Organizing Your Life Together	133
Travel and Adventure	133
Seasonal Adjustments	134
Daily Encouragement	135

MARRIAGE PROTECTION AND WISDOM

Setting Boundaries	138
Avoiding Temptation	138
Guarding Your Heart	139
Wisdom in Marriage	140
Discernment in Relationships	141
Avoiding Divorce	141
Getting Godly Counsel	142
Learning from Other Couples	143
Marriage Mentoring	144
Investing in Your Marriage	144
Never Giving Up	145
Fighting for Your Marriage	146
Covenant Keeping	147
Growing Old Together	147
Leaving a Marriage Legacy	148
Marriage and Eternity	149

INTRODUCTION

WHEN GOD DESIGNED MARRIAGE, HE HAD YOU IN MIND

Marriage wasn't an afterthought in the mind of the Almighty—it was His masterpiece! From the very beginning, in the garden where perfection met purpose, God looked at His creation and declared, "It is not good for man to be alone." In that divine moment, He established the first institution on earth, crafting a covenant so powerful that heaven itself would use it as the ultimate picture of Christ's love for His church.

But here's what somebody needs to understand: God didn't just create marriage and walk away. He left us a blueprint, a divine manual filled with wisdom, guidance, and supernatural power to build relationships that don't just survive—they thrive! Every struggle you face, every season you navigate, every breakthrough you need has already been addressed in the pages of Scripture.

THIS ISN'T JUST ANOTHER MARRIAGE BOOK—THIS IS YOUR ROADMAP TO VICTORY.

For too long, couples have stumbled through marriage without the proper tools, trying to build lasting love on shifting sand instead of the solid rock of God's Word. The enemy has convinced too many that good marriages are accidents of fate, that lasting love is reserved for the lucky few, that your relationship is destined to be ordinary. But that's a lie from the pit of hell! Your marriage was designed for greatness. You were created for connection that transcends the temporary and touches the eternal. The same God who holds the stars in place wants to hold your marriage together. The same power that raised Christ from the dead is available to resurrect dead dreams, restore broken trust, and revive passion that circumstances tried to kill.

THE MARRIAGE TOPICAL BIBLE places that power directly in your hands.

Within these pages, you'll discover 181 life-changing topics and over 2,000 carefully selected scriptures that speak directly to every aspect of your marriage journey. Whether you're newlyweds writing your love story or seasoned couples rewriting chapters that need redemption, God's Word has something to say about your situation.

Need wisdom for communication that heals instead of hurts? It's here. Seeking restoration after betrayal has shattered trust? These scriptures will guide you home. Fighting for intimacy in a world full of distractions? God's design for passionate, pure love awaits your discovery. Struggling with roles, responsibilities, or simply learning to love sacrificially? Every answer flows from the heart of heaven to the pages you're about to read.

This isn't surface-level inspiration—this is surgical precision. Each topic has been crafted to cut through confusion and deliver biblical truth that transforms. From the foundational principles that establish godly marriages to the practical wisdom that sustains them through every season, you'll find supernatural solutions for natural problems.

Your marriage is worth fighting for. Your love story deserves God's best. And your relationship has the potential to become a living testimony of heaven's love on earth.

Get ready for breakthrough. Get ready for restoration. Get ready to discover what happens when two hearts surrender to God's perfect plan for marriage.

FOUNDATIONAL MARRIAGE TOPICS

God's Design for Marriage

And the Lord God said, It is not good that the man should be alone; I will make him an help meet for him. Genesis 2:18

And the Lord God caused a deep sleep to fall upon Adam, and he slept: and he took one of his ribs, and closed up the flesh instead thereof; And the rib, which the Lord God had taken from man, made he a woman, and brought her unto the man. And Adam said, This is now bone of my bones, and flesh of my flesh: she shall be called Woman, because she was taken out of Man. Therefore shall a man leave his father and his mother, and shall cleave unto his wife: and they shall be one flesh. Genesis 2:21-24

So God created man in his own image, in the image of God created he him; male and female created he them. And God blessed them, and God said unto them, Be fruitful, and multiply, and replenish the earth, and subdue it. Genesis 1:27-28

Marriage is not finding the right person, but being the right person. It's not a 50-50 proposition; it's 100-100. - Anonymous

Have ye not read, that he which made them at the beginning made them male and female, And said, For this cause shall a man leave father and mother, and shall cleave to his wife: and they twain shall be one flesh? Wherefore they are no more twain, but one flesh. What therefore God hath joined together, let not man put asunder. Matthew 19:4-6

But from the beginning of the creation God made them male and female. For this cause shall a man leave his father and mother, and cleave to his wife; And they twain shall be one flesh: so then they are no more twain, but one flesh. What therefore God hath joined together, let not man put asunder. Mark 10:6-8

Marriage is honourable in all, and the bed undefiled: but whoremongers and adulterers God will judge. Hebrews 13:4

The Purpose of Marriage

And the Lord God said, It is not good that the man should be alone; I will make him an help meet for him. Genesis 2:18

That they may teach the young women to be sober, to love their husbands, to love their children, To be discreet, chaste, keepers at home, good, obedient to their own husbands, that the word of God be not blasphemed. Titus 2:4-5

Husbands, love your wives, even as Christ also loved the church, and gave himself for it; That he might sanctify and cleanse it with the washing of water by the word, That he might present it to himself a glorious church, not having spot, or wrinkle, or any such thing; but that it should be holy and without blemish. So ought men to love their wives as their own bodies. He that loveth his wife loveth himself. Ephesians 5:25-28

The purpose of marriage is not happiness but holiness.
God uses marriage to make us holy more than to make us happy.
- Gary Thomas

Two are better than one; because they have a good reward for their labour. For if they fall, the one will lift up his fellow: but woe to him that is alone when he falleth; for he hath not another to help him up. Again, if two lie together, then they have heat: but how can one be warm alone? And if one prevail against him, two shall withstand him; and a threefold cord is not quickly broken. Ecclesiastes 4:9-12

Live joyfully with the wife whom thou lovest all the days of the life of thy vanity, which he hath given thee under the sun, all the days of thy vanity: for that is thy portion in this life, and in thy labour which thou takest under the sun. Ecclesiastes 9:9

Marriage as a Covenant

Yet ye say, Wherefore? Because the Lord hath been witness between thee and the wife of thy youth, against whom thou hast dealt treacherously: yet is she thy companion, and the wife of thy covenant. And did not he make one? Yet had he the residue of the spirit. And wherefore one? That he might seek a godly seed. Therefore take heed to your spirit, and let none deal treacherously against the wife of his youth. For the Lord, the God of Israel, saith that he hateth putting away: for one covereth violence with his garment, saith the Lord of hosts: therefore take heed to your spirit, that ye deal not treacherously. Malachi 2:14-16

My covenant will I not break, nor alter the thing that is gone out of my lips. Psalms 89:34

He hath remembered his covenant for ever, the word which he commanded to a thousand generations. Psalms 105:8

And I will establish my covenant between me and thee and thy seed after thee in their generations for an everlasting covenant, to be a God unto thee, and to thy seed after thee. Genesis 17:7

Marriage is not a contract between two people, but a sacred covenant between two people and God. - Dave Meurer

Neither shall they take for their wives a widow, nor her that is put away: but they shall take maidens of the seed of the house of Israel, or a widow that had a priest before. Ezekiel 44:22

One Flesh Unity

Therefore shall a man leave his father and his mother, and shall cleave unto his wife: and they shall be one flesh. Genesis 2:24

So ought men to love their wives as their own bodies. He that loveth his wife loveth himself. For no man ever yet hated his own flesh; but nourisheth and cherisheth it, even as the Lord the church.
Ephesians 5:28-29

What therefore God hath joined together, let not man put asunder. Mark 10:9

The wife hath not power of her own body, but the husband: and likewise also the husband hath not power of his own body, but the wife. 1 Corinthians 7:4

And they twain shall be one flesh: so then they are no more twain, but one flesh. Mark 10:8

In marriage, being the right person is as important as finding the right person. - Wilbert Donald Gough

For this cause shall a man leave his father and mother, and shall be joined unto his wife, and they two shall be one flesh. This is a great mystery: but I speak concerning Christ and the church. Nevertheless let every one of you in particular so love his wife even as himself; and the wife see that she reverence her husband. Ephesians 5:31-33

Marriage Reflecting Christ and the Church

Wives, submit yourselves unto your own husbands, as unto the Lord. For the husband is the head of the wife, even as Christ is the head of the church: and he is the saviour of the body. Therefore as the church is subject unto Christ, so let the wives be to their own husbands in every thing. Husbands, love your wives, even as Christ also loved the church, and gave himself for it. Ephesians 5:22-25

This is a great mystery: but I speak concerning Christ and the church. Ephesians 5:32

For the husband is the head of the wife, even as Christ is the head of the church: and he is the saviour of the body. Ephesians 5:23

And gave himself for it; That he might sanctify and cleanse it with the washing of water by the word, That he might present it to himself a glorious church, not having spot, or wrinkle, or any such thing; but that it should be holy and without blemish. Ephesians 5:26-27

Marriage is God's way of illustrating the relationship between Christ and His church. - Anonymous

So ought men to love their wives as their own bodies. He that loveth his wife loveth himself. For no man ever yet hated his own flesh; but nourisheth and cherisheth it, even as the Lord the church: For we are members of his body, of his flesh, and of his bones.
Ephesians 5:28-30

God's Heart for Marriage

And the Lord God said, It is not good that the man should be alone; I will make him an help meet for him. Genesis 2:18

And God blessed them, and God said unto them, Be fruitful, and multiply, and replenish the earth, and subdue it. Genesis 1:28

For I know the thoughts that I think toward you, saith the Lord, thoughts of peace, and not of evil, to give you an expected end.
Jeremiah 29:11

For as a young man marrieth a virgin, so shall thy sons marry thee: and as the bridegroom rejoiceth over the bride, so shall thy God rejoice over thee. Isaiah 62:5

Marriage is God's idea. He designed it, He officiated at the first one, and He has never changed His mind about it. - Gary Smalley

Let thy fountain be blessed: and rejoice with the wife of thy youth. Let her be as the loving hind and pleasant roe; let her breasts satisfy thee at all times; and be thou ravished always with her love. Proverbs 5:18-19

House and riches are the inheritance of fathers: and a prudent wife is from the Lord. Proverbs 19:14

Marriage Before the Fall

And they were both naked, the man and his wife, and were not ashamed. Genesis 2:25

And the Lord God planted a garden eastward in Eden; and there he put the man whom he had formed. Genesis 2:8

And the Lord God took the man, and put him into the garden of Eden to dress it and to keep it. Genesis 2:15

And out of the ground the Lord God formed every beast of the field, and every fowl of the air; and brought them unto Adam to see what he would call them: and whatsoever Adam called every living creature, that was the name thereof. Genesis 2:19

Before sin entered the world, marriage was perfect - free from shame, guilt, or conflict. This gives us a picture of what God intends for marriage. - Henry Cloud

And Adam gave names to all cattle, and to the fowl of the air, and to every beast of the field; but for Adam there was not found an help meet for him. Genesis 2:20

And the Lord God said, It is not good that the man should be alone; I will make him an help meet for him. Genesis 2:18

The Sacred Nature of Marriage

Marriage is honourable in all, and the bed undefiled: but whoremongers and adulterers God will judge. Hebrews 13:4

What therefore God hath joined together, let not man put asunder. Matthew 19:6

But from the beginning of the creation God made them male and female. Mark 10:6

For this cause shall a man leave his father and mother, and cleave to his wife; And they twain shall be one flesh: so then they are no more twain, but one flesh. Mark 10:7-8

Marriage is the most sacred relationship between two people that can possibly exist on earth. - Pat Robertson

Wherefore they are no more twain, but one flesh. What therefore God hath joined together, let not man put asunder. Matthew 19:6

Let marriage be held in honor among all, and let the marriage bed be undefiled, for God will judge the sexually immoral and adulterous. Hebrews 13:4

Marriage as God's First Institution

And the Lord God said, It is not good that the man should be alone; I will make him an help meet for him. Genesis 2:18

Therefore shall a man leave his father and his mother, and shall cleave unto his wife: and they shall be one flesh. Genesis 2:24

And God blessed them, and God said unto them, Be fruitful, and multiply, and replenish the earth, and subdue it. Genesis 1:28

So God created man in his own image, in the image of God created he him; male and female created he them. Genesis 1:27

Marriage was the first institution established by God. It preceded government, the church, and every other human institution.
- James Dobson

And the Lord God caused a deep sleep to fall upon Adam, and he slept: and he took one of his ribs, and closed up the flesh instead thereof; And the rib, which the Lord God had taken from man, made he a woman, and brought her unto the man. Genesis 2:21-22

And Adam said, This is now bone of my bones, and flesh of my flesh: she shall be called Woman, because she was taken out of Man. Genesis 2:23

Divine Blessing on Marriage

And God blessed them, and God said unto them, Be fruitful, and multiply, and replenish the earth, and subdue it. Genesis 1:28

The Lord thy God shall bless thee in all thine increase, and in all the works of thine hands, therefore thou shalt surely rejoice. Deuteronomy 16:15

Except the Lord build the house, they labour in vain that build it: except the Lord keep the city, the watchman waketh but in vain. Psalms 127:1

Lo, children are an heritage of the Lord: and the fruit of the womb is his reward. As arrows are in the hand of a mighty man; so are children of the youth. Happy is the man that hath his quiver full of them: they shall not be ashamed, but they shall speak with the enemies in the gate. Psalms 127:3-5

When God joins two people in marriage, He blesses them with His presence, His power, and His provision. - Anonymous

Blessed is every one that feareth the Lord; that walketh in his ways. For thou shalt eat the labour of thine hands: happy shalt thou be, and it shall be well with thee. Thy wife shall be as a fruitful vine by the sides of thine house: thy children like olive plants round about thy table. Behold, that thus shall the man be blessed that feareth the Lord. Psalms 128:1-4

The blessing of the Lord, it maketh rich, and he addeth no sorrow with it. Proverbs 10:22

Marriage and God's Glory

Whether therefore ye eat, or drink, or whatsoever ye do, do all to the glory of God. 1 Corinthians 10:31

And whatsoever ye do in word or deed, do all in the name of the Lord Jesus, giving thanks to God and the Father by him. Colossians 3:17

For ye are bought with a price: therefore glorify God in your body, and in your spirit, which are God's. 1 Corinthians 6:20

Let your light so shine before men, that they may see your good works, and glorify your Father which is in heaven. Matthew 5:16

A godly marriage is one of the most powerful testimonies to the glory of God on earth. - John Piper

Herein is my Father glorified, that ye bear much fruit; so shall ye be my disciples. John 15:8

But let it be the hidden man of the heart, in that which is not corruptible, even the ornament of a meek and quiet spirit, which is in the sight of God of great price. 1 Peter 3:4

The Eternal Perspective of Marriage

For in the resurrection they neither marry, nor are given in marriage, but are as the angels of God in heaven. Matthew 22:30

But from the beginning of the creation God made them male and female. Mark 10:6

And Jesus answering said unto them, The children of this world marry, and are given in marriage: But they which shall be accounted worthy to obtain that world, and the resurrection from the dead, neither marry, nor are given in marriage. Luke 20:34-35

For we know that if our earthly house of this tabernacle were dissolved, we have a building of God, an house not made with hands, eternal in the heavens. 2 Corinthians 5:1

Marriage is temporal, but the love we learn in marriage prepares us for eternal love with Christ. - Randy Alcorn

While we look not at the things which are seen, but at the things which are not seen: for the things which are seen are temporal; but the things which are not seen are eternal. 2 Corinthians 4:18

Set your affection on things above, not on things on the earth. Colossians 3:2

Marriage as Partnership

Two are better than one; because they have a good reward for their labour. For if they fall, the one will lift up his fellow: but woe to him that is alone when he falleth; for he hath not another to help him up. Again, if two lie together, then they have heat: but how can one be warm alone? And if one prevail against him, two shall withstand him; and a threefold cord is not quickly broken. Ecclesiastes 4:9-12

And the Lord God said, It is not good that the man should be alone; I will make him an help meet for him. Genesis 2:18

Iron sharpeneth iron; so a man sharpeneth the countenance of his friend. Proverbs 27:17

Be ye not unequally yoked together with unbelievers: for what fellowship hath righteousness with unrighteousness? and what communion hath light with darkness? 2 Corinthians 6:14

Marriage is a partnership where both partners work together toward common goals under God's direction. - Gary Chapman

As every man hath received the gift, even so minister the same one to another, as good stewards of the manifold grace of God.
1 Peter 4:10

Bear ye one another's burdens, and so fulfil the law of Christ. Galatians 6:2

Choosing a Godly Spouse

Be ye not unequally yoked together with unbelievers: for what fellowship hath righteousness with unrighteousness? and what communion hath light with darkness? 2 Corinthians 6:14

House and riches are the inheritance of fathers: and a prudent wife is from the Lord. Proverbs 19:14

Who can find a virtuous woman? for her price is far above rubies. Proverbs 31:10

A virtuous woman is a crown to her husband: but she that maketh ashamed is as rottenness in his bones. Proverbs 12:4

The most important decision you'll make after choosing Christ is choosing your spouse. Choose wisely. - Anonymous

Favour is deceitful, and beauty is vain: but a woman that feareth the Lord, she shall be praised. Proverbs 31:30

Whoso findeth a wife findeth a good thing, and obtaineth favour of the Lord. Proverbs 18:22

Preparing for Marriage

Trust in the Lord with all thine heart; and lean not unto thine own understanding. In all thy ways acknowledge him, and he shall direct thy paths. Proverbs 3:5-6

Commit thy way unto the Lord; trust also in him; and he shall bring it to pass. Psalms 37:5

But seek ye first the kingdom of God, and his righteousness; and all these things shall be added unto you. Matthew 6:33

Delight thyself also in the Lord; and he shall give thee the desires of thine heart. Psalms 37:4

The best preparation for marriage is becoming the person God wants you to be. - Gary Thomas

And let us not be weary in well doing: for in due season we shall reap, if we faint not. Galatians 6:9

Study to shew thyself approved unto God, a workman that needeth not to be ashamed, rightly dividing the word of truth. 2 Timothy 2:15
The Wedding Covenant

For this cause shall a man leave his father and mother, and shall be joined unto his wife, and they two shall be one flesh. Ephesians 5:31

What therefore God hath joined together, let not man put asunder. Mark 10:9

Yet ye say, Wherefore? Because the Lord hath been witness between thee and the wife of thy youth, against whom thou hast dealt treacherously: yet is she thy companion, and the wife of thy covenant. Malachi 2:14

And I will betroth thee unto me for ever; yea, I will betroth thee unto me in righteousness, and in judgment, and in lovingkindness, and in mercies. Hosea 2:19

A wedding is a day; a marriage is a lifetime. The covenant made at the altar must be lived out daily. - Anonymous

My covenant will I not break, nor alter the thing that is gone out of my lips. Psalms 89:34

When thou vowest a vow unto God, defer not to pay it; for he hath no pleasure in fools: pay that which thou hast vowed. Ecclesiastes 5:4

The Wedding Covenant

For this cause shall a man leave his father and mother, and shall be joined unto his wife, and they two shall be one flesh. Ephesians 5:31

What therefore God hath joined together, let not man put asunder. Mark 10:9

Yet ye say, Wherefore? Because the Lord hath been witness between thee and the wife of thy youth, against whom thou hast dealt treacherously: yet is she thy companion, and the wife of thy covenant. Malachi 2:14

And I will betroth thee unto me for ever; yea, I will betroth thee unto me in righteousness, and in judgment, and in lovingkindness, and in mercies. Hosea 2:19

A wedding is a day; a marriage is a lifetime. The covenant made at the altar must be lived out daily. - Anonymous

My covenant will I not break, nor alter the thing that is gone out of my lips. Psalms 89:34

When thou vowest a vow unto God, defer not to pay it; for he hath no pleasure in fools: pay that which thou hast vowed. Ecclesiastes 5:4

Leaving and Cleaving

Therefore shall a man leave his father and his mother, and shall cleave unto his wife: and they shall be one flesh. Genesis 2:24

For this cause shall a man leave his father and mother, and cleave to his wife; And they twain shall be one flesh: so then they are no more twain, but one flesh. Mark 10:7-8

And said, For this cause shall a man leave father and mother, and shall cleave to his wife: and they twain shall be one flesh? Matthew 19:5

Can two walk together, except they be agreed? Amos 3:3
Leaving means releasing dependence on parents; cleaving means establishing a new primary relationship with your spouse.
- Gary Smalley

And Ruth said, Intreat me not to leave thee, or to return from following after thee: for whither thou goest, I will go; and where thou lodgest, I will lodge: thy people shall be my people, and thy God my God. Ruth 1:16

Therefore if any man be in Christ, he is a new creature: old things are passed away; behold, all things are become new. 2 Corinthians 5:17

Establishing a Christian Home

As for me and my house, we will serve the Lord. Joshua 24:15

And these words, which I command thee this day, shall be in thine heart: And thou shalt teach them diligently unto thy children, and shalt talk of them when thou sittest in thine house, and when thou walkest by the way, and when thou liest down, and when thou risest up. Deuteronomy 6:6-7

Except the Lord build the house, they labour in vain that build it: except the Lord keep the city, the watchman waketh but in vain. Psalms 127:1

Through wisdom is an house builded; and by understanding it is established: And by knowledge shall the chambers be filled with all precious and pleasant riches. Proverbs 24:3-4

A Christian home is where Christ is head, love is the law, and service is the privilege. - Anonymous

The just man walketh in his integrity: his children are blessed after him. Proverbs 20:7

But if any provide not for his own, and specially for those of his own house, he hath denied the faith, and is worse than an infidel. 1 Timothy 5:8

Marriage and God's Will

And we know that all things work together for good to them that love God, to them who are the called according to his purpose. Romans 8:28

For I know the thoughts that I think toward you, saith the Lord, thoughts of peace, and not of evil, to give you an expected end. Jeremiah 29:11

Trust in the Lord with all thine heart; and lean not unto thine own understanding. In all thy ways acknowledge him, and he shall direct thy paths. Proverbs 3:5-6

Commit thy works unto the Lord, and thy thoughts shall be established. Proverbs 16:3

God's will for your marriage is that it brings glory to Him and demonstrates His love to the world. - Gary Thomas

And be not conformed to this world: but be ye transformed by the renewing of your mind, that ye may prove what is that good, and acceptable, and perfect, will of God. Romans 12:2

A man's heart deviseth his way: but the Lord directeth his steps. Proverbs 16:9

The Sanctity of the Marriage Bed

Marriage is honourable in all, and the bed undefiled: but whoremongers and adulterers God will judge. Hebrews 13:4

Let the husband render unto the wife due benevolence: and likewise also the wife unto the husband. The wife hath not power of her own body, but the husband: and likewise also the husband hath not power of his own body, but the wife. 1 Corinthians 7:3-4

Defraud ye not one the other, except it be with consent for a time, that ye may give yourselves to fasting and prayer; and come together again, that Satan tempt you not for your incontinency. 1 Corinthians 7:5

Let thy fountain be blessed: and rejoice with the wife of thy youth. Let her be as the loving hind and pleasant roe; let her breasts satisfy thee at all times; and be thou ravished always with her love. Proverbs 5:18-19

Sexual intimacy in marriage is God's gift to be enjoyed with purity, passion, and mutual pleasure. - Ed Wheat

Drink waters out of thine own cistern, and running waters out of thine own well. Proverbs 5:15

Let marriage be held in honor among all, and let the marriage bed be undefiled, for God will judge the sexually immoral and adulterous. Hebrews 13:4

Marriage and Holiness

For this is the will of God, even your sanctification, that ye should abstain from fornication: That every one of you should know how to possess his vessel in sanctification and honour.
1 Thessalonians 4:3-4

But as he which hath called you is holy, so be ye holy in all manner of conversation; Because it is written, Be ye holy; for I am holy.
1 Peter 1:15-16

And be not conformed to this world: but be ye transformed by the renewing of your mind, that ye may prove what is that good, and acceptable, and perfect, will of God. Romans 12:2

Follow peace with all men, and holiness, without which no man shall see the Lord. Hebrews 12:14

Marriage is designed by God to make us holy, not just happy.
- Gary Thomas

That he might sanctify and cleanse it with the washing of water by the word, That he might present it to himself a glorious church, not having spot, or wrinkle, or any such thing; but that it should be holy and without blemish. Ephesians 5:26-27

Husbands, love your wives, even as Christ also loved the church, and gave himself for it. Ephesians 5:25

Growing Together Spiritually

Iron sharpeneth iron; so a man sharpeneth the countenance of his friend. Proverbs 27:17

But grow in grace, and in the knowledge of our Lord and Saviour Jesus Christ. To him be glory both now and for ever. Amen.
2 Peter 3:18

As every man hath received the gift, even so minister the same one to another, as good stewards of the manifold grace of God.
1 Peter 4:10

And let us consider one another to provoke unto love and to good works. Hebrews 10:24

A couple that prays together, stays together. Spiritual growth in marriage requires intentional effort from both spouses. - Anonymous

Can two walk together, except they be agreed? Amos 3:3
Where there is no vision, the people perish: but he that keepeth the law, happy is he. Proverbs 29:18

Marriage and God's Faithfulness

Know therefore that the Lord thy God, he is God, the faithful God, which keepeth covenant and mercy with them that love him and keep his commandments to a thousand generations.
Deuteronomy 7:9

It is of the Lord's mercies that we are not consumed, because his compassions fail not. They are new every morning: great is thy faithfulness. Lamentations 3:22-23

If we believe not, yet he abideth faithful: he cannot deny himself. 2 Timothy 2:13

God is faithful, by whom ye were called unto the fellowship of his Son Jesus Christ our Lord. 1 Corinthians 1:9

God's faithfulness to His covenant with us is the model for our faithfulness in marriage. - John Piper

Let us hold fast the profession of our faith without wavering; for he is faithful that promised. Hebrews 10:23

Thy mercy, O Lord, is in the heavens; and thy faithfulness reacheth unto the clouds. Psalms 36:5

The Beauty of Marriage

And God saw every thing that he had made, and, behold, it was very good. And the evening and the morning were the sixth day. Genesis 1:31

He hath made every thing beautiful in his time: also he hath set the world in their heart, so that no man can find out the work that God maketh from the beginning to the end. Ecclesiastes 3:11

Favour is deceitful, and beauty is vain: but a woman that feareth the Lord, she shall be praised. Proverbs 31:30

As the lily among thorns, so is my love among the daughters. Song of Solomon 2:2

True beauty in marriage comes not from physical appearance alone, but from the character of Christ shining through both spouses.
- Elisabeth Elliot

But let it be the hidden man of the heart, in that which is not corruptible, even the ornament of a meek and quiet spirit, which is in the sight of God of great price. 1 Peter 3:4

Strength and honour are her clothing; and she shall rejoice in time to come. Proverbs 31:25

Marriage and Divine Love

Beloved, let us love one another: for love is of God; and every one that loveth is born of God, and knoweth God. He that loveth not knoweth not God; for God is love. 1 John 4:7-8

Herein is love, not that we loved God, but that he loved us, and sent his Son to be the propitiation for our sins. Beloved, if God so loved us, we ought also to love one another. 1 John 4:10-11

And we have known and believed the love that God hath to us. God is love; and he that dwelleth in love dwelleth in God, and God in him. 1 John 4:16

But God commendeth his love toward us, in that, while we were yet sinners, Christ died for us. Romans 5:8

Human love in marriage is meant to reflect divine love - unconditional, sacrificial, and eternal. - Max Lucado

We love him, because he first loved us. 1 John 4:19
And above all these things put on charity, which is the bond of perfectness. Colossians 3:14

God's Protection Over Marriage

The name of the Lord is a strong tower: the righteous runneth into it, and is safe. Proverbs 18:10

He that dwelleth in the secret place of the most High shall abide under the shadow of the Almighty. I will say of the Lord, He is my refuge and my fortress: my God; in him will I trust. Psalms 91:1-2

But the Lord is faithful, who shall stablish you, and keep you from evil. 2 Thessalonians 3:3

The Lord shall preserve thee from all evil: he shall preserve thy soul. The Lord shall preserve thy going out and thy coming in from this time forth, and even for evermore. Psalms 121:7-8

God places a hedge of protection around marriages that honor Him and seek His will. - James Dobson

And I will betroth thee unto me for ever; yea, I will betroth thee unto me in righteousness, and in judgment, and in lovingkindness, and in mercies. Hosea 2:19

Submit yourselves therefore to God. Resist the devil, and he will flee from you. James 4:7

Marriage as Ministry

As every man hath received the gift, even so minister the same one to another, as good stewards of the manifold grace of God. 1 Peter 4:10

And whatsoever ye do in word or deed, do all in the name of the Lord Jesus, giving thanks to God and the Father by him. Colossians 3:17

For we are his workmanship, created in Christ Jesus unto good works, which God hath before ordained that we should walk in them. Ephesians 2:10

But as we were allowed of God to be put in trust with the gospel, even so we speak; not as pleasing men, but God, which trieth our hearts. 1 Thessalonians 2:4

Marriage is not just about your happiness; it's about your ministry to each other and to the world. - Gary Thomas

Use hospitality one to another without grudging. 1 Peter 4:9
Bear ye one another's burdens, and so fulfil the law of Christ. Galatians 6:2

The Joy of Marriage

Whoso findeth a wife findeth a good thing, and obtaineth favour of the Lord. Proverbs 18:22

Let thy fountain be blessed: and rejoice with the wife of thy youth. Proverbs 5:18

Live joyfully with the wife whom thou lovest all the days of the life of thy vanity, which he hath given thee under the sun, all the days of thy vanity: for that is thy portion in this life, and in thy labour which thou takest under the sun. Ecclesiastes 9:9

Thou wilt shew me the path of life: in thy presence is fulness of joy; at thy right hand there are pleasures for evermore. Psalms 16:11

A joyful marriage is not one without problems, but one where problems are faced together with hope in God. - Tim Keller

And these things write we unto you, that your joy may be full. 1 John 1:4

For the kingdom of God is not meat and drink; but righteousness, and peace, and joy in the Holy Ghost. Romans 14:17

Marriage and God's Presence

For where two or three are gathered together in my name, there am I in the midst of them. Matthew 18:20

Draw nigh to God, and he will draw nigh to you. Cleanse your hands, ye sinners; and purify your hearts, ye double minded. James 4:8
And I will dwell among the children of Israel, and will be their God. Exodus 29:45

Behold, the tabernacle of God is with men, and he will dwell with them, and they shall be his people, and God himself shall be with them, and be their God. Revelation 21:3

When Christ is invited into a marriage, He doesn't just attend the wedding - He inhabits the relationship. - Max Lucado

Teaching them to observe all things whatsoever I have commanded you: and, lo, I am with you alway, even unto the end of the world. Amen. Matthew 28:20

In all thy ways acknowledge him, and he shall direct thy paths. Proverbs 3:6

Honoring Marriage

Marriage is honourable in all, and the bed undefiled: but whoremongers and adulterers God will judge. Hebrews 13:4
Honour all men. Love the brotherhood. Fear God. Honour the king. 1 Peter 2:17

Render therefore to all their dues: tribute to whom tribute is due; custom to whom custom; fear to whom fear; honour to whom honour. Romans 13:7

Nevertheless let every one of you in particular so love his wife even as himself; and the wife see that she reverence her husband. Ephesians 5:33

We honor marriage by the way we speak about it, treat it, and live it out before others. - Dennis Rainey

Let marriage be held in honor among all, and let the marriage bed be undefiled, for God will judge the sexually immoral and adulterous. Hebrews 13:4

Thy wife shall be as a fruitful vine by the sides of thine house: thy children like olive plants round about thy table. Psalms 128:3

ROLES AND RESPONSIBILITIES

Biblical Roles in Marriage

But I would have you know, that the head of every man is Christ; and the head of the woman is the man; and the head of Christ is God.
1 Corinthians 11:3

Wives, submit yourselves unto your own husbands, as unto the Lord. For the husband is the head of the wife, even as Christ is the head of the church: and he is the saviour of the body. Ephesians 5:22-23

Husbands, love your wives, even as Christ also loved the church, and gave himself for it. Ephesians 5:25

Nevertheless let every one of you in particular so love his wife even as himself; and the wife see that she reverence her husband. Ephesians 5:33

Biblical roles in marriage are not about superiority or inferiority, but about order, function, and mutual love and respect.
- John MacArthur

Wives, submit yourselves unto your own husbands, as it is fit in the Lord. Husbands, love your wives, and be not bitter against them. Colossians 3:18-19

Likewise, ye wives, be in subjection to your own husbands; that, if any obey not the word, they also may without the word be won by the conversation of the wives. 1 Peter 3:1

Loving Your Wife as Christ Loved the Church

Husbands, love your wives, even as Christ also loved the church, and gave himself for it; That he might sanctify and cleanse it with the washing of water by the word, That he might present it to himself a glorious church, not having spot, or wrinkle, or any such thing;

but that it should be holy and without blemish. So ought men to love their wives as their own bodies. He that loveth his wife loveth himself. Ephesians 5:25-28

Greater love hath no man than this, that a man lay down his life for his friends. John 15:13

But God commendeth his love toward us, in that, while we were yet sinners, Christ died for us. Romans 5:8

For no man ever yet hated his own flesh; but nourisheth and cherisheth it, even as the Lord the church. Ephesians 5:29

The measure of a husband's love is not what he feels, but what he does. Christ's love was demonstrated through sacrifice.
- Anonymous

Hereby perceive we the love of God, because he laid down his life for us: and we ought to lay down our lives for the brethren. 1 John 3:16

And walk in love, as Christ also hath loved us, and hath given himself for us an offering and a sacrifice to God for a sweetsmelling savour. Ephesians 5:2

The Husband as Head

But I would have you know, that the head of every man is Christ; and the head of the woman is the man; and the head of Christ is God.
1 Corinthians 11:3

For the husband is the head of the wife, even as Christ is the head of the church: and he is the saviour of the body. Ephesians 5:23

And he is the head of the body, the church: who is the beginning, the firstborn from the dead; that in all things he might have the preeminence. Colossians 1:18

Now I praise you, brethren, that ye remember me in all things, and keep the ordinances, as I delivered them to you. 1 Corinthians 11:2

Headship is not dictatorship but loving leadership that serves, protects, and provides for the family. - R.C. Sproul

Nevertheless let every one of you in particular so love his wife even as himself; and the wife see that she reverence her husband. Ephesians 5:33

But I suffer not a woman to teach, nor to usurp authority over the man, but to be in silence. 1 Timothy 2:12

Servant Leadership in Marriage

But Jesus called them unto him, and said, Ye know that the princes of the Gentiles exercise dominion over them, and they that are great exercise authority upon them. But it shall not be so among you: but whosoever will be great among you, let him be your minister; And whosoever will be chief among you, let him be your servant: Even as the Son of man came not to be ministered unto, but to minister, and to give his life a ransom for many. Matthew 20:25-28

If I then, your Lord and Master, have washed your feet; ye also ought to wash one another's feet. For I have given you an example, that ye should do as I have done to you. John 13:14-15

Let this mind be in you, which was also in Christ Jesus: Who, being in the form of God, thought it not robbery to be equal with God: But made himself of no reputation, and took upon him the form of a servant, and was made in the likeness of men. Philippians 2:5-7

True leadership in marriage means serving your wife's highest good, not demanding your own way. - Gary Thomas

Likewise, ye husbands, dwell with them according to knowledge, giving honour unto the wife, as unto the weaker vessel, and as being heirs together of the grace of life; that your prayers be not hindered. 1 Peter 3:7

And whosoever of you will be the chiefest, shall be servant of all. Mark 10:44

The Wife as Helper

And the Lord God said, It is not good that the man should be alone; I will make him an help meet for him. Genesis 2:18

Who can find a virtuous woman? for her price is far above rubies. The heart of her husband doth safely trust in her, so that he shall have no need of spoil. She will do him good and not evil all the days of her life. Proverbs 31:10-12

Every wise woman buildeth her house: but the foolish plucketh it down with her hands. Proverbs 14:1

House and riches are the inheritance of fathers: and a prudent wife is from the Lord. Proverbs 19:14

A helper is not a subordinate but a complement - someone who provides what is lacking to make the team complete. - John Piper

A virtuous woman is a crown to her husband: but she that maketh ashamed is as rottenness in his bones. Proverbs 12:4

The heart of her husband doth safely trust in her, so that he shall have no need of spoil. Proverbs 31:11

Submission in Marriage

Wives, submit yourselves unto your own husbands, as unto the Lord. For the husband is the head of the wife, even as Christ is the head of the church: and he is the saviour of the body. Therefore as the church is subject unto Christ, so let the wives be to their own husbands in every thing. Ephesians 5:22-24

Wives, submit yourselves unto your own husbands, as it is fit in the Lord. Colossians 3:18

Likewise, ye wives, be in subjection to your own husbands; that, if any obey not the word, they also may without the word be won by the conversation of the wives; While they behold your chaste conversation coupled with fear. 1 Peter 3:1-2

Submitting yourselves one to another in the fear of God. Ephesians 5:21

Biblical submission is not about inferiority but about order and respect in the marriage relationship. - John MacArthur

Let this mind be in you, which was also in Christ Jesus: Who, being in the form of God, thought it not robbery to be equal with God: But made himself of no reputation, and took upon him the form of a servant, and was made in the likeness of men. Philippians 2:5-7

Yea, all of you be subject one to another, and be clothed with humility: for God resisteth the proud, and giveth grace to the humble. 1 Peter 5:5

Mutual Submission

Submitting yourselves one to another in the fear of God. Ephesians 5:21

Be kindly affectioned one to another with brotherly love; in honour preferring one another. Romans 12:10

Let nothing be done through strife or vainglory; but in lowliness of mind let each esteem other better than themselves. Look not every man on his own things, but every man also on the things of others. Philippians 2:3-4

And be ye kind one to another, tenderhearted, forgiving one another, even as God for Christ's sake hath forgiven you. Ephesians 4:32

Mutual submission means both spouses put the other's needs above their own in a spirit of love and service. - Gary Thomas

Let this mind be in you, which was also in Christ Jesus. Philippians 2:5

By love serve one another. Galatians 5:13

Honoring Your Husband

Nevertheless let every one of you in particular so love his wife even as himself; and the wife see that she reverence her husband. Ephesians 5:33

Likewise, ye wives, be in subjection to your own husbands; that, if any obey not the word, they also may without the word be won by the conversation of the wives; While they behold your chaste conversation coupled with fear. 1 Peter 3:1-2

The heart of her husband doth safely trust in her, so that he shall have no need of spoil. She will do him good and not evil all the days of her life. Proverbs 31:11-12

Her husband is known in the gates, when he sitteth among the elders of the land. Proverbs 31:23

A wife honors her husband by respecting his leadership, supporting his decisions, and speaking well of him to others.
- Emerson Eggerichs

Render therefore to all their dues: tribute to whom tribute is due; custom to whom custom; fear to whom fear; honour to whom honour. Romans 13:7

Honour all men. Love the brotherhood. Fear God. Honour the king. 1 Peter 2:17

Respecting Your Spouse

Nevertheless let every one of you in particular so love his wife even as himself; and the wife see that she reverence her husband. Ephesians 5:33

Likewise, ye husbands, dwell with them according to knowledge, giving honour unto the wife, as unto the weaker vessel, and as being heirs together of the grace of life; that your prayers be not hindered. 1 Peter 3:7

Be kindly affectioned one to another with brotherly love; in honour preferring one another. Romans 12:10

Let nothing be done through strife or vainglory; but in lowliness of mind let each esteem other better than themselves. Philippians 2:3

Respect is the foundation of love. Without respect, love becomes mere sentiment. - Emerson Eggerichs

Honour all men. Love the brotherhood. Fear God. Honour the king. 1 Peter 2:17

And be ye kind one to another, tenderhearted, forgiving one another, even as God for Christ's sake hath forgiven you. Ephesians 4:32

Protecting Your Marriage

Above all else, guard your heart, for everything you do flows from it. Proverbs 4:23

Be sober, be vigilant; because your adversary the devil, as a roaring lion, walketh about, seeking whom he may devour. 1 Peter 5:8

Submit yourselves therefore to God. Resist the devil, and he will flee from you. James 4:7

Finally, my brethren, be strong in the Lord, and in the power of his might. Put on the whole armour of God, that ye may be able to stand against the wiles of the devil. Ephesians 6:10-11

A marriage that is not protected will not be preserved. Build walls against temptation and bridges toward each other. - Gary Thomas

Watch and pray, that ye enter not into temptation: the spirit indeed is willing, but the flesh is weak. Matthew 26:41

Marriage is honourable in all, and the bed undefiled: but whoremongers and adulterers God will judge. Hebrews 13:4

Providing for Your Family

But if any provide not for his own, and specially for those of his own house, he hath denied the faith, and is worse than an infidel. 1 Timothy 5:8

And that ye study to be quiet, and to do your own business, and to work with your own hands, as we commanded you; That ye may walk honestly toward them that are without, and that ye may have lack of nothing. 1 Thessalonians 4:11-12

For even when we were with you, this we commanded you, that if any would not work, neither should he eat. 2 Thessalonians 3:10

In the sweat of thy face shalt thou eat bread, till thou return unto the ground; for out of it wast thou taken: for dust thou art, and unto dust shalt thou return. Genesis 3:19

A man's primary responsibility is to provide for his family, not just financially but emotionally and spiritually as well. - John MacArthur
She looketh well to the ways of her household, and eateth not the bread of idleness. Proverbs 31:27

Be thou diligent to know the state of thy flocks, and look well to thy herds. Proverbs 27:23

Nurturing in Marriage

But we were gentle among you, even as a nurse cherisheth her children. 1 Thessalonians 2:7

For no man ever yet hated his own flesh; but nourisheth and cherisheth it, even as the Lord the church. Ephesians 5:29

As one whom his mother comforteth, so will I comfort you; and ye shall be comforted in Jerusalem. Isaiah 66:13

And be ye kind one to another, tenderhearted, forgiving one another, even as God for Christ's sake hath forgiven you. Ephesians 4:32

Nurturing in marriage means creating an environment where both spouses can grow and flourish. - Gary Chapman

Comfort yourselves together, and edify one another, even as also ye do. 1 Thessalonians 5:11

Bear ye one another's burdens, and so fulfil the law of Christ. Galatians 6:2

Leading Your Family Spiritually

And, ye fathers, provoke not your children to wrath: but bring them up in the nurture and admonition of the Lord. Ephesians 6:4

And these words, which I command thee this day, shall be in thine heart: And thou shalt teach them diligently unto thy children, and shalt talk of them when thou sittest in thine house, and when thou walkest by the way, and when thou liest down, and when thou risest up. Deuteronomy 6:6-7

As for me and my house, we will serve the Lord. Joshua 24:15
Train up a child in the way he should go: and when he is old, he will not depart from it. Proverbs 22:6

Spiritual leadership in the home is not about being perfect but about being faithful to point your family toward God. - Dennis Rainey
The just man walketh in his integrity: his children are blessed after him. Proverbs 20:7

And he shall turn the heart of the fathers to the children, and the heart of the children to their fathers, lest I come and smite the earth with a curse. Malachi 4:6

Supporting Your Spouse's Dreams

Let nothing be done through strife or vainglory; but in lowliness of mind let each esteem other better than themselves. Look not every man on his own things, but every man also on the things of others. Philippians 2:3-4

Bear ye one another's burdens, and so fulfil the law of Christ. Galatians 6:2

And let us consider one another to provoke unto love and to good works. Hebrews 10:24

Two are better than one; because they have a good reward for their labour. Ecclesiastes 4:9

A loving spouse helps their partner become all that God has called them to be. - Gary Thomas

Iron sharpeneth iron; so a man sharpeneth the countenance of his friend. Proverbs 27:17

As every man hath received the gift, even so minister the same one to another, as good stewards of the manifold grace of God. 1 Peter 4:10

BEING A GODLY EXAMPLE

Let your light so shine before men, that they may see your good works, and glorify your Father which is in heaven. Matthew 5:16

In all things shewing thyself a pattern of good works: in doctrine shewing uncorruptness, gravity, sincerity. Titus 2:7

Be thou an example of the believers, in word, in conversation, in charity, in spirit, in faith, in purity. 1 Timothy 4:12

Those things, which ye have both learned, and received, and heard, and seen in me, do: and the God of peace shall be with you. Philippians 4:9

Your life is the most powerful sermon your family will ever hear.
- Anonymous

The just man walketh in his integrity: his children are blessed after him. Proverbs 20:7

And thou shalt be called, The repairer of the breach, The restorer of paths to dwell in. Isaiah 58:12

Responsibility and Accountability

So then every one of us shall give account of himself to God. Romans 14:12

Moreover it is required in stewards, that a man be found faithful. 1 Corinthians 4:2

But I say unto you, That every idle word that men shall speak, they shall give account thereof in the day of judgment. Matthew 12:36

For we must all appear before the judgment seat of Christ; that every one may receive the things done in his body, according to that he hath done, whether it be good or bad. 2 Corinthians 5:10

In marriage, we are accountable to God for how we treat the spouse He has given us. - Gary Thomas

And unto whomsoever much is given, of him shall be much required: and to whom men have committed much, of him they will ask the more. Luke 12:48

As every man hath received the gift, even so minister the same one to another, as good stewards of the manifold grace of God. 1 Peter 4:10

Stewardship in Marriage

Moreover it is required in stewards, that a man be found faithful. 1 Corinthians 4:2

As every man hath received the gift, even so minister the same one to another, as good stewards of the manifold grace of God.
1 Peter 4:10

And the Lord said, Who then is that faithful and wise steward, whom his lord shall make ruler over his household, to give them their portion of meat in due season? Luke 12:42

For unto whomsoever much is given, of him shall be much required: and to whom men have committed much, of him they will ask the more. Luke 12:48

Marriage is a stewardship from God. We are called to be faithful managers of the relationship He has entrusted to us. - Dennis Rainey
But it is required in stewards, that a man be found faithful.
1 Corinthians 4:2

Render unto Caesar the things which are Caesar's, and unto God the things that are God's. Mark 12:17

Being Your Spouse's Best Friend

A friend loveth at all times, and a brother is born for adversity. Proverbs 17:17

A man that hath friends must shew himself friendly: and there is a friend that sticketh closer than a brother. Proverbs 18:24

Iron sharpeneth iron; so a man sharpeneth the countenance of his friend. Proverbs 27:17

This is my beloved, and this is my friend, O daughters of Jerusalem. Song of Solomon 5:16

The best marriages are between people who choose to be best friends for life. - Gary Chapman

Faithful are the wounds of a friend; but the kisses of an enemy are deceitful. Proverbs 27:6

Greater love hath no man than this, that a man lay down his life for his friends. John 15:13

Encouraging Your Partner

Therefore comfort yourselves together, and edify one another, even as also ye do. 1 Thessalonians 5:11

Let no corrupt communication proceed out of your mouth, but that which is good to the use of edifying, that it may minister grace unto the hearers. Ephesians 4:29

And let us consider one another to provoke unto love and to good works. Hebrews 10:24

Wherefore lift up the hands which hang down, and the feeble knees. Hebrews 12:12

Encouragement is oxygen to the soul. Your words can breathe life into your spouse's dreams. - John Maxwell

Pleasant words are as an honeycomb, sweet to the soul, and health to the bones. Proverbs 16:24

A word fitly spoken is like apples of gold in pictures of silver. Proverbs 25:11

Building Up Your Spouse

Let no corrupt communication proceed out of your mouth, but that which is good to the use of edifying, that it may minister grace unto the hearers. Ephesians 4:29

Wherefore comfort yourselves together, and edify one another, even as also ye do. 1 Thessalonians 5:11

Iron sharpeneth iron; so a man sharpeneth the countenance of his friend. Proverbs 27:17

And let us consider one another to provoke unto love and to good works. Hebrews 10:24

Your spouse should be more confident because of your words, not less confident. - Gary Chapman

All things are lawful for me, but all things are not expedient: all things are lawful for me, but all things edify not. 1 Corinthians 10:23

But he that prophesieth speaketh unto men to edification, and exhortation, and comfort. 1 Corinthians 14:3

LOVE AND INTIMACY

Unconditional Love in Marriage

Charity suffereth long, and is kind; charity envieth not; charity vaunteth not itself, is not puffed up, Doth not behave itself unseemly, seeketh not her own, is not easily provoked, thinketh no evil; Rejoiceth not in iniquity, but rejoiceth in the truth; Beareth all things, believeth all things, hopeth all things, endureth all things. Charity never faileth. 1 Corinthians 13:4-8

And above all these things put on charity, which is the bond of perfectness. Colossians 3:14

But God commendeth his love toward us, in that, while we were yet sinners, Christ died for us. Romans 5:8

Herein is love, not that we loved God, but that he loved us, and sent his Son to be the propitiation for our sins. 1 John 4:10

Love is not a feeling; it's a decision. It's a commitment to seek the highest good of another person. - Gary Chapman

We love him, because he first loved us. 1 John 4:19

And this commandment have we from him, That he who loveth God love his brother also. 1 John 4:21

Expressing Love Daily

And walk in love, as Christ also hath loved us, and hath given himself for us an offering and a sacrifice to God for a sweetsmelling savour. Ephesians 5:2

Let all your things be done with charity. 1 Corinthians 16:14

And above all these things put on charity, which is the bond of perfectness. Colossians 3:14

But whoso hath this world's good, and seeth his brother have need, and shutteth up his bowels of compassion from him, how dwelleth the love of God in him? My little children, let us not love in word, neither in tongue; but in deed and in truth. 1 John 3:17-18

Love is expressed more in what we do than in what we say. Actions speak louder than words. - Anonymous

Be kindly affectioned one to another with brotherly love; in honour preferring one another. Romans 12:10

And let us consider one another to provoke unto love and to good works. Hebrews 10:24

Love Languages in Marriage

A word fitly spoken is like apples of gold in pictures of silver. Proverbs 25:11

Pleasant words are as an honeycomb, sweet to the soul, and health to the bones. Proverbs 16:24

The tongue of the wise useth knowledge aright: but the mouth of fools poureth out foolishness. Proverbs 15:2

And be ye kind one to another, tenderhearted, forgiving one another, even as God for Christ's sake hath forgiven you. Ephesians 4:32

Every person has a primary way of feeling loved. Discover your spouse's love language and speak it fluently. - Gary Chapman

Let no corrupt communication proceed out of your mouth, but that which is good to the use of edifying, that it may minister grace unto the hearers. Ephesians 4:29

For he that will love life, and see good days, let him refrain his tongue from evil, and his lips that they speak no guile. 1 Peter 3:10

Romantic Love

Behold, thou art fair, my love; behold, thou art fair; thou hast doves' eyes. Song of Solomon 1:15

How fair is thy love, my sister, my spouse! how much better is thy love than wine! and the smell of thine ointments than all spices! Song of Solomon 4:10

My beloved spake, and said unto me, Rise up, my love, my fair one, and come away. For, lo, the winter is past, the rain is over and gone; The flowers appear on the earth; the time of the singing of birds is come, and the voice of the turtle is heard in our land. Song of Solomon 2:10-12

Set me as a seal upon thine heart, as a seal upon thine arm: for love is strong as death; jealousy is cruel as the grave: the coals thereof are coals of fire, which hath a most vehement flame. Many waters cannot quench love, neither can the floods drown it: if a man would give all the substance of his house for love, it would utterly be contemned. Song of Solomon 8:6-7

Romance is not just for dating; it's essential for a thriving marriage. Keep courting your spouse throughout your life together.
- Gary Chapman

Let thy fountain be blessed: and rejoice with the wife of thy youth. Let her be as the loving hind and pleasant roe; let her breasts satisfy thee at all times; and be thou ravished always with her love. Proverbs 5:18-19

I am my beloved's, and my beloved is mine: he feedeth among the lilies. Song of Solomon 6:3

Intimate Communication

Behold, thou art fair, my love; behold, thou art fair; thou hast doves' eyes within thy locks: thy hair is as a flock of goats, that appear from mount Gilead. Song of Solomon 4:1

This is my beloved, and this is my friend, O daughters of Jerusalem. Song of Solomon 5:16

Let your speech be alway with grace, seasoned with salt, that ye may know how ye ought to answer every man. Colossians 4:6

Pleasant words are as an honeycomb, sweet to the soul, and health to the bones. Proverbs 16:24

Intimate communication goes beyond surface conversation to share hearts, dreams, fears, and hopes. - Gary Smalley

A word fitly spoken is like apples of gold in pictures of silver. Proverbs 25:11

Let no corrupt communication proceed out of your mouth, but that which is good to the use of edifying, that it may minister grace unto the hearers. Ephesians 4:29

Physical Intimacy in Marriage

Marriage is honourable in all, and the bed undefiled: but whoremongers and adulterers God will judge. Hebrews 13:4

Let the husband render unto the wife due benevolence: and likewise also the wife unto the husband. The wife hath not power of her own body, but the husband: and likewise also the husband hath not power of his own body, but the wife. Defraud ye not one the other, except it be with consent for a time, that ye may give yourselves to fasting and prayer; and come together again, that Satan tempt you not for your incontinency. 1 Corinthians 7:3-5

Let thy fountain be blessed: and rejoice with the wife of thy youth. Let her be as the loving hind and pleasant roe; let her breasts satisfy thee at all times; and be thou ravished always with her love. Proverbs 5:18-19

Drink waters out of thine own cistern, and running waters out of thine own well. Proverbs 5:15

Physical intimacy in marriage is God's gift for pleasure, bonding, and procreation within the covenant relationship. - Ed Wheat

Therefore shall a man leave his father and his mother, and shall cleave unto his wife: and they shall be one flesh. Genesis 2:24

Let marriage be held in honor among all, and let the marriage bed be undefiled, for God will judge the sexually immoral and adulterous. Hebrews 13:4

Emotional Intimacy

And they were both naked, the man and his wife, and were not ashamed. Genesis 2:25

Bear ye one another's burdens, and so fulfil the law of Christ. Galatians 6:2

Rejoice with them that do rejoice, and weep with them that weep. Romans 12:15

And be ye kind one to another, tenderhearted, forgiving one another, even as God for Christ's sake hath forgiven you. Ephesians 4:32

Emotional intimacy requires vulnerability, trust, and the willingness to be known completely by another person. - Henry Cloud

A friend loveth at all times, and a brother is born for adversity. Proverbs 17:17

Confess your faults one to another, and pray one for another, that ye may be healed. The effectual fervent prayer of a righteous man availeth much. James 5:16

Spiritual Intimacy

For where two or three are gathered together in my name, there am I in the midst of them. Matthew 18:20

Can two walk together, except they be agreed? Amos 3:3

Again I say unto you, That if two of you shall agree on earth as touching any thing that they shall ask, it shall be done for them of my Father which is in heaven. Matthew 18:19

Iron sharpeneth iron; so a man sharpeneth the countenance of his friend. Proverbs 27:17

The deepest intimacy in marriage occurs when a couple worships God together and grows spiritually as one. - Dennis Rainey

And let us consider one another to provoke unto love and to good works: Not forsaking the assembling of ourselves together, as the manner of some is; but exhorting one another: and so much the more, as ye see the day approaching. Hebrews 10:24-25

But grow in grace, and in the knowledge of our Lord and Saviour Jesus Christ. To him be glory both now and for ever. Amen. 2 Peter 3:18

Growing in Love

But grow in grace, and in the knowledge of our Lord and Saviour Jesus Christ. To him be glory both now and for ever. Amen.
2 Peter 3:18

And this I pray, that your love may abound yet more and more in knowledge and in all judgment. Philippians 1:9

But the path of the just is as the shining light, that shineth more and more unto the perfect day. Proverbs 4:18

And beside this, giving all diligence, add to your faith virtue; and to virtue knowledge; And to knowledge temperance; and to temperance patience; and to patience godliness; And to godliness brotherly kindness; and to brotherly kindness charity. 2 Peter 1:5-7

Love is not a static emotion but a growing choice that deepens through commitment and shared experiences. - Gary Thomas

Charity never faileth: but whether there be prophecies, they shall fail; whether there be tongues, they shall cease; whether there be knowledge, it shall vanish away. 1 Corinthians 13:8

And above all these things put on charity, which is the bond of perfectness. Colossians 3:14

Sacrificial Love

Greater love hath no man than this, that a man lay down his life for his friends. John 15:13

Husbands, love your wives, even as Christ also loved the church, and gave himself for it. Ephesians 5:25

But God commendeth his love toward us, in that, while we were yet sinners, Christ died for us. Romans 5:8

Hereby perceive we the love of God, because he laid down his life for us: and we ought to lay down our lives for the brethren. 1 John 3:16

True love is not about getting but about giving. It seeks the highest good of the beloved, even at personal cost. - Max Lucado

And walk in love, as Christ also hath loved us, and hath given himself for us an offering and a sacrifice to God for a sweetsmelling savour. Ephesians 5:2

Let nothing be done through strife or vainglory; but in lowliness of mind let each esteem other better than themselves. Philippians 2:3

Passionate Love

Set me as a seal upon thine heart, as a seal upon thine arm: for love is strong as death; jealousy is cruel as the grave: the coals thereof are coals of fire, which hath a most vehement flame.
Song of Solomon 8:6

Many waters cannot quench love, neither can the floods drown it: if a man would give all the substance of his house for love, it would utterly be contemned. Song of Solomon 8:7

I am my beloved's, and his desire is toward me.
Song of Solomon 7:10

My beloved is mine, and I am his: he feedeth among the lilies.
Song of Solomon 2:16

Passion in marriage is both physical and emotional - a deep desire for your spouse that goes beyond mere attraction. - Tommy Nelson
Let thy fountain be blessed: and rejoice with the wife of thy youth.
Proverbs 5:18

How fair and how pleasant art thou, O love, for delights!
Song of Solomon 7:6

Tender Affection

Be kindly affectioned one to another with brotherly love; in honour preferring one another. Romans 12:10

And be ye kind one to another, tenderhearted, forgiving one another, even as God for Christ's sake hath forgiven you. Ephesians 4:32

But we were gentle among you, even as a nurse cherisheth her children. 1 Thessalonians 2:7

For no man ever yet hated his own flesh; but nourisheth and cherisheth it, even as the Lord the church. Ephesians 5:29

Tender affection is the gentle touch, the soft word, the caring look that says 'you matter to me.' - Gary Chapman

A soft answer turneth away wrath: but grievous words stir up anger. Proverbs 15:1

Pleasant words are as an honeycomb, sweet to the soul, and health to the bones. Proverbs 16:24

Demonstrating Love

My little children, let us not love in word, neither in tongue; but in deed and in truth. 1 John 3:18

But whoso hath this world's good, and seeth his brother have need, and shutteth up his bowels of compassion from him, how dwelleth the love of God in him? 1 John 3:17

And walk in love, as Christ also hath loved us, and hath given himself for us an offering and a sacrifice to God for a sweetsmelling savour. Ephesians 5:2

By this shall all men know that ye are my disciples, if ye have love one to another. John 13:35

Love is not just a feeling; it's an action. It's demonstrated through what we do, not just what we say. - Gary Chapman

Even so faith, if it hath not works, is dead, being alone. James 2:17

For God is not unrighteous to forget your work and labour of love, which ye have shewed toward his name, in that ye have ministered to the saints, and do minister. Hebrews 6:10

Love Through Actions

And whatsoever ye do in word or deed, do all in the name of the Lord Jesus, giving thanks to God and the Father by him. Colossians 3:17

Let all your things be done with charity. 1 Corinthians 16:14

And let us not be weary in well doing: for in due season we shall reap, if we faint not. Galatians 6:9

She looketh well to the ways of her household, and eateth not the bread of idleness. Proverbs 31:27

Love is a verb. It requires action, effort, and intentionality to be expressed effectively. - Gary Smalley

Her children arise up, and call her blessed; her husband also, and he praiseth her. Proverbs 31:28

She will do him good and not evil all the days of her life. Proverbs 31:12

Speaking Words of Love

Pleasant words are as an honeycomb, sweet to the soul, and health to the bones. Proverbs 16:24

A word fitly spoken is like apples of gold in pictures of silver. Proverbs 25:11

Death and life are in the power of the tongue: and they that love it shall eat the fruit thereof. Proverbs 18:21

Let no corrupt communication proceed out of your mouth, but that which is good to the use of edifying, that it may minister grace unto the hearers. Ephesians 4:29

Words have power to heal or to hurt. Choose words that build up your spouse and strengthen your marriage. - Gary Chapman

Let your speech be alway with grace, seasoned with salt, that ye may know how ye ought to answer every man. Colossians 4:6

The tongue of the wise useth knowledge aright: but the mouth of fools poureth out foolishness. Proverbs 15:2

Love in Difficult Times

Charity suffereth long, and is kind; charity envieth not; charity vaunteth not itself, is not puffed up, Doth not behave itself unseemly, seeketh not her own, is not easily provoked, thinketh no evil; Rejoiceth not in iniquity, but rejoiceth in the truth; Beareth all things, believeth all things, hopeth all things, endureth all things.
1 Corinthians 13:4-7

A friend loveth at all times, and a brother is born for adversity. Proverbs 17:17

And we know that all things work together for good to them that love God, to them who are the called according to his purpose.
Romans 8:28

These things I have spoken unto you, that in me ye might have peace. In the world ye shall have tribulation: but be of good cheer; I have overcome the world. John 16:33

True love is not tested in good times but proven in difficult times. It's then that love chooses to stay. - Gary Thomas

Many waters cannot quench love, neither can the floods drown it: if a man would give all the substance of his house for love, it would utterly be contemned. Song of Solomon 8:7

For I am persuaded, that neither death, nor life, nor angels, nor principalities, nor powers, nor things present, nor things to come, Nor height, nor depth, nor any other creature, shall be able to separate us from the love of God, which is in Christ Jesus our Lord.
Romans 8:38-39

Rekindling Romance

I will arise now, and go about the city in the streets, and in the broad ways I will seek him whom my soul loveth: I sought him, but I found him not. Song of Solomon 3:2

The voice of my beloved! behold, he cometh leaping upon the mountains, skipping upon the hills. Song of Solomon 2:8

Until the day break, and the shadows flee away, I will get me to the mountain of myrrh, and to the hill of frankincense.
Song of Solomon 4:6

Draw me, we will run after thee: the king hath brought me into his chambers: we will be glad and rejoice in thee, we will remember thy love more than wine: the upright love thee. Song of Solomon 1:4

Romance doesn't end with the wedding; it requires ongoing cultivation and intentional effort throughout marriage.
- Gary Chapman

Nevertheless I have somewhat against thee, because thou hast left thy first love. Remember therefore from whence thou art fallen, and repent, and do the first works. Revelation 2:4-5

My beloved spake, and said unto me, Rise up, my love, my fair one, and come away. Song of Solomon 2:10

Celebrating Your Spouse

Her children arise up, and call her blessed; her husband also, and he praiseth her. Many daughters have done virtuously, but thou excellest them all. Proverbs 31:28-29

Let another man praise thee, and not thine own mouth; a stranger, and not thine own lips. Proverbs 27:2

Whoso findeth a wife findeth a good thing, and obtaineth favour of the Lord. Proverbs 18:22

Live joyfully with the wife whom thou lovest all the days of the life of thy vanity, which he hath given thee under the sun, all the days of thy vanity: for that is thy portion in this life, and in thy labour which thou takest under the sun. Ecclesiastes 9:9

Celebrating your spouse means recognizing their worth, acknowledging their contributions, and expressing gratitude regularly. - Gary Chapman

In every thing give thanks: for this is the will of God in Christ Jesus concerning you. 1 Thessalonians 5:18

Giving thanks always for all things unto God and the Father in the name of our Lord Jesus Christ. Ephesians 5:20

Intimate Friendship

A friend loveth at all times, and a brother is born for adversity. Proverbs 17:17

A man that hath friends must shew himself friendly: and there is a friend that sticketh closer than a brother. Proverbs 18:24

Iron sharpeneth iron; so a man sharpeneth the countenance of his friend. Proverbs 27:17

This is my beloved, and this is my friend, O daughters of Jerusalem. Song of Solomon 5:16

The strongest marriages are built on intimate friendship - knowing each other deeply and genuinely enjoying each other's company. - John Gottman

Faithful are the wounds of a friend; but the kisses of an enemy are deceitful. Proverbs 27:6

Two are better than one; because they have a good reward for their labour. Ecclesiastes 4:9

The Song of Solomon Marriage

Behold, thou art fair, my love; behold, thou art fair; thou hast doves' eyes. Song of Solomon 1:15

I am the rose of Sharon, and the lily of the valleys. As the lily among thorns, so is my love among the daughters. Song of Solomon 2:1-2

My beloved is mine, and I am his: he feedeth among the lilies.
Song of Solomon 2:16

Set me as a seal upon thine heart, as a seal upon thine arm: for love is strong as death; jealousy is cruel as the grave: the coals thereof are coals of fire, which hath a most vehement flame.
Song of Solomon 8:6

The Song of Solomon gives us God's picture of passionate, romantic, committed love between a husband and wife
. - Tommy Nelson

How fair is thy love, my sister, my spouse! how much better is thy love than wine! and the smell of thine ointments than all spices!
Song of Solomon 4:10

I am my beloved's, and his desire is toward me.
Song of Solomon 7:10

COMMUNICATION

Godly Communication in Marriage

Let your speech be alway with grace, seasoned with salt, that ye may know how ye ought to answer every man. Colossians 4:6

Let no corrupt communication proceed out of your mouth, but that which is good to the use of edifying, that it may minister grace unto the hearers. Ephesians 4:29

A soft answer turneth away wrath: but grievous words stir up anger. Proverbs 15:1

Pleasant words are as an honeycomb, sweet to the soul, and health to the bones. Proverbs 16:24

Communication is to marriage what blood is to the body. When it stops flowing, the relationship dies. - Anonymous

The heart of the righteous studieth to answer: but the mouth of the wicked poureth out evil things. Proverbs 15:28

Wherefore, my beloved brethren, let every man be swift to hear, slow to speak, slow to wrath. James 1:19

Speaking Truth in Love

But speaking the truth in love, may grow up into him in all things, which is the head, even Christ. Ephesians 4:15

Wherefore putting away lying, speak every man truth with his neighbour: for we are members one of another. Ephesians 4:25

These are the things that ye shall do; Speak ye every man the truth to his neighbour; execute the judgment of truth and peace in your gates. Zechariah 8:16

Faithful are the wounds of a friend; but the kisses of an enemy are deceitful. Proverbs 27:6

Truth without love is brutality; love without truth is sentimentality. In marriage, we need both truth and love. - Warren Wiersbe

The lip of truth shall be established for ever: but a lying tongue is but for a moment. Proverbs 12:19

Better is open rebuke than secret love. Proverbs 27:5

Listening with Understanding

Wherefore, my beloved brethren, let every man be swift to hear, slow to speak, slow to wrath. James 1:19

He that answereth a matter before he heareth it, it is folly and shame unto him. Proverbs 18:13

The heart of the prudent getteth knowledge; and the ear of the wise seeketh knowledge. Proverbs 18:15

If any of you lack wisdom, let him ask of God, that giveth to all men liberally, and upbraideth not; and it shall be given him. James 1:5

God gave us two ears and one mouth so we would listen twice as much as we speak. - Anonymous

A fool hath no delight in understanding, but that his heart may discover itself. Proverbs 18:2

The simple believeth every word: but the prudent man looketh well to his going. Proverbs 14:15

Healing Words

Pleasant words are as an honeycomb, sweet to the soul, and health to the bones. Proverbs 16:24

A word fitly spoken is like apples of gold in pictures of silver. Proverbs 25:11

The tongue of the wise is health. Proverbs 12:18

There is that speaketh like the piercings of a sword: but the tongue of the wise is health. Proverbs 12:18

Words have the power to heal wounds, restore hope, and breathe life into a discouraged heart. - Gary Chapman

Death and life are in the power of the tongue: and they that love it shall eat the fruit thereof. Proverbs 18:21

Let no corrupt communication proceed out of your mouth, but that which is good to the use of edifying, that it may minister grace unto the hearers. Ephesians 4:29

Avoiding Harmful Speech

Let no corrupt communication proceed out of your mouth, but that which is good to the use of edifying, that it may minister grace unto the hearers. Ephesians 4:29

But now ye also put off all these; anger, wrath, malice, blasphemy, filthy communication out of your mouth. Colossians 3:8

A soft answer turneth away wrath: but grievous words stir up anger. Proverbs 15:1

He that keepeth his mouth keepeth his life: but he that openeth wide his lips shall have destruction. Proverbs 13:3
Words that tear down, criticize harshly, or attack character have no place in a godly marriage. - John Gottman

Be not rash with thy mouth, and let not thine heart be hasty to utter any thing before God: for God is in heaven, and thou upon earth: therefore let thy words be few. Ecclesiastes 5:2

Set a watch, O Lord, before my mouth; keep the door of my lips. Psalms 141:3

Conflict Resolution

Moreover if thy brother shall trespass against thee, go and tell him his fault between thee and him alone: if he shall hear thee, thou hast gained thy brother. Matthew 18:15

Be ye angry, and sin not: let not the sun go down upon your wrath. Ephesians 4:26

And be ye kind one to another, tenderhearted, forgiving one another, even as God for Christ's sake hath forgiven you. Ephesians 4:32

If it be possible, as much as lieth in you, live peaceably with all men. Romans 12:18

Conflict is inevitable in marriage, but fighting fair and seeking resolution honors God and strengthens the relationship.
- Gary Chapman

A soft answer turneth away wrath: but grievous words stir up anger. Proverbs 15:1

Blessed are the peacemakers: for they shall be called the children of God. Matthew 5:9

Arguing Righteously

Be ye angry, and sin not: let not the sun go down upon your wrath. Ephesians 4:26

But I say unto you, That whosoever is angry with his brother without a cause shall be in danger of the judgment. Matthew 5:22

A wrathful man stirreth up strife: but he that is slow to anger appeaseth strife. Proverbs 15:18

Wherefore, my beloved brethren, let every man be swift to hear, slow to speak, slow to wrath: For the wrath of man worketh not the righteousness of God. James 1:19-20

It's possible to address issues and disagreements without sinning. Focus on the problem, not attacking the person. - Neil Clark Warren
The beginning of strife is as when one letteth out water: therefore leave off contention, before it be meddled with. Proverbs 17:14

A fool's wrath is presently known: but a prudent man covereth shame. Proverbs 12:16

Gentle Responses

A soft answer turneth away wrath: but grievous words stir up anger. Proverbs 15:1

But the fruit of the Spirit is love, joy, peace, longsuffering, gentleness, goodness, faith, Meekness, temperance: against such there is no law. Galatians 5:22-23

And the servant of the Lord must not strive; but be gentle unto all men, apt to teach, patient. 2 Timothy 2:24

Let your moderation be known unto all men. The Lord is at hand. Philippians 4:5

A gentle response can defuse anger and open the door to understanding and resolution. - Gary Smalley

Take my yoke upon you, and learn of me; for I am meek and lowly in heart: and ye shall find rest unto your souls. Matthew 11:29

But we were gentle among you, even as a nurse cherisheth her children. 1 Thessalonians 2:7

Encouraging Words

Therefore comfort yourselves together, and edify one another, even as also ye do. 1 Thessalonians 5:11

Let no corrupt communication proceed out of your mouth, but that which is good to the use of edifying, that it may minister grace unto the hearers. Ephesians 4:29

And let us consider one another to provoke unto love and to good works. Hebrews 10:24

Wherefore lift up the hands which hang down, and the feeble knees. Hebrews 12:12

Your words can be the wind beneath your spouse's wings or the anchor that holds them down. Choose encouragement.
- John Maxwell

Pleasant words are as an honeycomb, sweet to the soul, and health to the bones. Proverbs 16:24

A word fitly spoken is like apples of gold in pictures of silver. Proverbs 25:11

Speaking Blessings

And God blessed them, and God said unto them, Be fruitful, and multiply, and replenish the earth, and subdue it. Genesis 1:28

The blessing of the Lord, it maketh rich, and he addeth no sorrow with it. Proverbs 10:22

And he lifted up his hands, and blessed them. Luke 24:50

Bless them which persecute you: bless, and curse not. Romans 12:14

Speaking blessings over your spouse calls forth God's best in their life and releases His favor upon them. - Dutch Sheets

Her children arise up, and call her blessed; her husband also, and he praiseth her. Proverbs 31:28

And Jabez called on the God of Israel, saying, Oh that thou wouldest bless me indeed, and enlarge my coast, and that thine hand might be with me, and that thou wouldest keep me from evil, that it may not grieve me! And God granted him that which he requested.
1 Chronicles 4:10

Communication During Crisis

A word fitly spoken is like apples of gold in pictures of silver. Proverbs 25:11

Be not rash with thy mouth, and let not thine heart be hasty to utter any thing before God: for God is in heaven, and thou upon earth: therefore let thy words be few. Ecclesiastes 5:2

Wherefore, my beloved brethren, let every man be swift to hear, slow to speak, slow to wrath. James 1:19

The heart of the righteous studieth to answer: but the mouth of the wicked poureth out evil things. Proverbs 15:28

In times of crisis, our words can either escalate the situation or bring peace and stability. - Gary Chapman

A time to keep silence, and a time to speak. Ecclesiastes 3:7

Even a fool, when he holdeth his peace, is counted wise: and he that shutteth his lips is esteemed a man of understanding.
Proverbs 17:28

Vulnerable Sharing

Confess your faults one to another, and pray one for another, that ye may be healed. The effectual fervent prayer of a righteous man availeth much. James 5:16

Bear ye one another's burdens, and so fulfil the law of Christ. Galatians 6:2

And they were both naked, the man and his wife, and were not ashamed. Genesis 2:25

If we walk in the light, as he is in the light, we have fellowship one with another, and the blood of Jesus Christ his Son cleanseth us from all sin. 1 John 1:7

Vulnerability in marriage creates intimacy. When we share our struggles, fears, and weaknesses, we invite deeper connection.
- Brené Brown

Faithful are the wounds of a friend; but the kisses of an enemy are deceitful. Proverbs 27:6

Two are better than one; because they have a good reward for their labour. For if they fall, the one will lift up his fellow.
Ecclesiastes 4:9-10

Active Listening

Wherefore, my beloved brethren, let every man be swift to hear, slow to speak, slow to wrath. James 1:19

He that answereth a matter before he heareth it, it is folly and shame unto him. Proverbs 18:13

The heart of the prudent getteth knowledge; and the ear of the wise seeketh knowledge. Proverbs 18:15

Give therefore thy servant an understanding heart to judge thy people, that I may discern between good and bad: for who is able to judge this thy so great a people? 1 Kings 3:9

Active listening means giving your full attention, seeking to understand before being understood. - Stephen Covey

A fool hath no delight in understanding, but that his heart may discover itself. Proverbs 18:2

If any of you lack wisdom, let him ask of God, that giveth to all men liberally, and upbraideth not; and it shall be given him. James 1:5

Non-verbal Communication

A merry heart maketh a cheerful countenance: but by sorrow of the heart the spirit is broken. Proverbs 15:13

Let your light so shine before men, that they may see your good works, and glorify your Father which is in heaven. Matthew 5:16

The light of the eyes rejoiceth the heart: and a good report maketh the bones fat. Proverbs 15:30

But let it be the hidden man of the heart, in that which is not corruptible, even the ornament of a meek and quiet spirit, which is in the sight of God of great price. 1 Peter 3:4

Studies show that 55% of communication is body language, 38% is tone of voice, and only 7% is words. - Albert Mehrabian

Pleasant words are as an honeycomb, sweet to the soul, and health to the bones. Proverbs 16:24

A soft answer turneth away wrath: but grievous words stir up anger. Proverbs 15:1

Restoring Communication

Come now, and let us reason together, saith the Lord: though your sins be as scarlet, they shall be as white as snow; though they be red like crimson, they shall be as wool. Isaiah 1:18

Therefore if thou bring thy gift to the altar, and there rememberest that thy brother hath ought against thee; Leave there thy gift before the altar, and go thy way; first be reconciled to thy brother, and then come and offer thy gift. Matthew 5:23-24

Moreover if thy brother shall trespass against thee, go and tell him his fault between thee and him alone: if he shall hear thee, thou hast gained thy brother. Matthew 18:15

And be ye kind one to another, tenderhearted, forgiving one another, even as God for Christ's sake hath forgiven you. Ephesians 4:32

When communication breaks down, the path to restoration requires humility, grace, and intentional effort from both spouses.
- Gary Chapman

If we confess our sins, he is faithful and just to forgive us our sins, and to cleanse us from all unrighteousness. 1 John 1:9

Brethren, if a man be overtaken in a fault, ye which are spiritual, restore such an one in the spirit of meekness; considering thyself, lest thou also be tempted. Galatians 6:1

FORGIVENESS AND HEALING

Forgiveness in Marriage

And be ye kind one to another, tenderhearted, forgiving one another, even as God for Christ's sake hath forgiven you. Ephesians 4:32

And when ye stand praying, forgive, if ye have ought against any: that your Father also which is in heaven may forgive you your trespasses. But if ye do not forgive, neither will your Father which is in heaven forgive your trespasses. Mark 11:25-26

Then came Peter to him, and said, Lord, how oft shall my brother sin against me, and I forgive him? till seven times? Jesus saith unto him, I say not unto thee, Until seven times: but, Until seventy times seven. Matthew 18:21-22

Forbearing one another, and forgiving one another, if any man have a quarrel against any: even as Christ forgave you, so also do ye. Colossians 3:13

Forgiveness is not a feeling; it's a decision. It's choosing to give up your right to hurt someone who has hurt you. - Anonymous
And forgive us our debts, as we forgive our debtors. Matthew 6:12

For if ye forgive men their trespasses, your heavenly Father will also forgive you: But if ye forgive not men their trespasses, neither will your Father forgive your trespasses. Matthew 6:14-15

Seeking Forgiveness

If we confess our sins, he is faithful and just to forgive us our sins, and to cleanse us from all unrighteousness. 1 John 1:9

He that covereth his sins shall not prosper: but whoso confesseth and forsaketh them shall have mercy. Proverbs 28:13

Therefore if thou bring thy gift to the altar, and there rememberest that thy brother hath ought against thee; Leave there thy gift before the altar, and go thy way; first be reconciled to thy brother, and then come and offer thy gift. Matthew 5:23-24

Confess your faults one to another, and pray one for another, that ye may be healed. The effectual fervent prayer of a righteous man availeth much. James 5:16

Pride goes before destruction, and an haughty spirit before a fall. - Proverbs 16:18

I acknowledged my sin unto thee, and mine iniquity have I not hid. I said, I will confess my transgressions unto the Lord; and thou forgavest the iniquity of my sin. Selah. Psalms 32:5

Only by pride cometh contention: but with the well advised is wisdom. Proverbs 13:10

Forgiving Deep Hurts

And be ye kind one to another, tenderhearted, forgiving one another, even as God for Christ's sake hath forgiven you. Ephesians 4:32

Then came Peter to him, and said, Lord, how oft shall my brother sin against me, and I forgive him? till seven times? Jesus saith unto him, I say not unto thee, Until seven times: but, Until seventy times seven. Matthew 18:21-22

Forbearing one another, and forgiving one another, if any man have a quarrel against any: even as Christ forgave you, so also do ye. Colossians 3:13

And when ye stand praying, forgive, if ye have ought against any: that your Father also which is in heaven may forgive you your trespasses. Mark 11:25

Forgiving deep hurts is not about minimizing the pain but about releasing the right to revenge and choosing healing. - Lewis Smedes
For if ye forgive men their trespasses, your heavenly Father will also forgive you: But if ye forgive not men their trespasses, neither will your Father forgive your trespasses. Matthew 6:14-15

And Jesus said, Father, forgive them; for they know not what they do. And they parted his raiment, and cast lots. Luke 23:34

Letting Go of the Past

Brethren, I count not myself to have apprehended: but this one thing I do, forgetting those things which are behind, and reaching forth unto those things which are before, I press toward the mark for the prize of the high calling of God in Christ Jesus. Philippians 3:13-14

Therefore if any man be in Christ, he is a new creature: old things are passed away; behold, all things are become new. 2 Corinthians 5:17

Remember ye not the former things, neither consider the things of old. Behold, I will do a new thing; now it shall spring forth; shall ye not know it? I will even make a way in the wilderness, and rivers in the desert. Isaiah 43:18-19

And their sins and iniquities will I remember no more. Hebrews 10:17

Letting go of the past doesn't mean forgetting lessons learned, but refusing to let past hurts poison present joy. - Joyce Meyer

As far as the east is from the west, so far hath he removed our transgressions from us. Psalms 103:12

But one thing I do, forgetting those things which are behind, and reaching forth unto those things which are before. Philippians 3:13

Healing from Betrayal

He healeth the broken in heart, and bindeth up their wounds. Psalms 147:3

The Lord is nigh unto them that are of a broken heart; and saveth such as be of a contrite spirit. Psalms 34:18

Come unto me, all ye that labour and are heavy laden, and I will give you rest. Matthew 11:28

He hath sent me to heal the brokenhearted, to preach deliverance to the captives, and recovering of sight to the blind, to set at liberty them that are bruised. Luke 4:18

Healing from betrayal is a process, not an event. It requires time, grace, and often professional help. - Henry Cloud

To appoint unto them that mourn in Zion, to give unto them beauty for ashes, the oil of joy for mourning, the garment of praise for the spirit of heaviness. Isaiah 61:3

And we know that all things work together for good to them that love God, to them who are the called according to his purpose. Romans 8:28

Restoring Trust

Moreover if thy brother shall trespass against thee, go and tell him his fault between thee and him alone: if he shall hear thee, thou hast gained thy brother. Matthew 18:15

If we confess our sins, he is faithful and just to forgive us our sins, and to cleanse us from all unrighteousness. 1 John 1:9

He that covereth his sins shall not prosper: but whoso confesseth and forsaketh them shall have mercy. Proverbs 28:13

Confess your faults one to another, and pray one for another, that ye may be healed. The effectual fervent prayer of a righteous man availeth much. James 5:16

Trust is like a mirror - once broken, it can be repaired, but you'll always see the cracks. However, God can restore what seems impossible. - Anonymous

Create in me a clean heart, O God; and renew a right spirit within me. Psalms 51:10

The steps of a good man are ordered by the Lord: and he delighteth in his way. Though he fall, he shall not be utterly cast down: for the Lord upholdeth him with his hand. Psalms 37:23-24

Overcoming Offense

Great peace have they which love thy law: and nothing shall offend them. Psalms 119:165

It is impossible but that offences will come: but woe unto him, through whom they come! Luke 17:1

A brother offended is harder to be won than a strong city: and their contentions are like the bars of a castle. Proverbs 18:19

And blessed is he, whosoever shall not be offended in me. Matthew 11:6

Offense is a trap that can destroy relationships. Choose to release offense and guard your heart from bitterness. - John Bevere

Above all else, guard your heart, for everything you do flows from it. Proverbs 4:23

Looking diligently lest any man fail of the grace of God; lest any root of bitterness springing up trouble you, and thereby many be defiled. Hebrews 12:15

Grace in Marriage

But he giveth more grace. Wherefore he saith, God resisteth the proud, but giveth grace unto the humble. James 4:6

And God is able to make all grace abound toward you; that ye, always having all sufficiency in all things, may abound to every good work. 2 Corinthians 9:8

For by grace are ye saved through faith; and that not of yourselves: it is the gift of God. Ephesians 2:8

Let us therefore come boldly unto the throne of grace, that we may obtain mercy, and find grace to help in time of need. Hebrews 4:16
Grace in marriage means giving your spouse what they need, not what they deserve. - Gary Thomas

But where sin abounded, grace did much more abound. Romans 5:20

And of his fulness have all we received, and grace for grace. John 1:16

Mercy in Relationships

But the mercy of the Lord is from everlasting to everlasting upon them that fear him, and his righteousness unto children's children. Psalms 103:17

It is of the Lord's mercies that we are not consumed, because his compassions fail not. They are new every morning: great is thy faithfulness. Lamentations 3:22-23

The Lord is merciful and gracious, slow to anger, and plenteous in mercy. Psalms 103:8

Blessed are the merciful: for they shall obtain mercy. Matthew 5:7

Mercy is not getting what you deserve; grace is getting what you don't deserve. Both are essential in marriage. - Max Lucado

Let us therefore come boldly unto the throne of grace, that we may obtain mercy, and find grace to help in time of need. Hebrews 4:16

But thou, O Lord, art a God full of compassion, and gracious, longsuffering, and plenteous in mercy and truth. Psalms 86:15

Second Chances

The steps of a good man are ordered by the Lord: and he delighteth in his way. Though he fall, he shall not be utterly cast down: for the Lord upholdeth him with his hand. Psalms 37:23-24

For a just man falleth seven times, and riseth up again: but the wicked shall fall into mischief. Proverbs 24:16

If we confess our sins, he is faithful and just to forgive us our sins, and to cleanse us from all unrighteousness. 1 John 1:9

And the Lord said unto me, Go yet, love a woman beloved of her friend, yet an adulteress, according to the love of the Lord toward the children of Israel, who look to other gods, and love flagons of wine. Hosea 3:1

God is the God of second chances, and marriage sometimes requires multiple chances for growth and restoration. - Chuck Swindoll

He hath not dealt with us after our sins; nor rewarded us according to our iniquities. Psalms 103:10

And their sins and iniquities will I remember no more. Hebrews 10:17

Healing Broken Hearts

He healeth the broken in heart, and bindeth up their wounds. Psalms 147:3

The Lord is nigh unto them that are of a broken heart; and saveth such as be of a contrite spirit. Psalms 34:18

The sacrifices of God are a broken spirit: a broken and a contrite heart, O God, thou wilt not despise. Psalms 51:17

To appoint unto them that mourn in Zion, to give unto them beauty for ashes, the oil of joy for mourning, the garment of praise for the spirit of heaviness. Isaiah 61:3

God specializes in healing broken hearts. He can restore what seems irreparably damaged. - Beth Moore

Come unto me, all ye that labour and are heavy laden, and I will give you rest. Matthew 11:28

Weeping may endure for a night, but joy cometh in the morning. Psalms 30:5

Restoration After Failure

Brethren, if a man be overtaken in a fault, ye which are spiritual, restore such an one in the spirit of meekness; considering thyself, lest thou also be tempted. Galatians 6:1

And the God of all grace, who hath called us unto his eternal glory by Christ Jesus, after that ye have suffered a while, make you perfect, stablish, strengthen, settle you. 1 Peter 5:10

If we confess our sins, he is faithful and just to forgive us our sins, and to cleanse us from all unrighteousness. 1 John 1:9

Create in me a clean heart, O God; and renew a right spirit within me. Psalms 51:10

Failure is not final when we have a God who specializes in restoration and redemption. - Tony Evans

Restore unto me the joy of thy salvation; and uphold me with thy free spirit. Psalms 51:12

Therefore if any man be in Christ, he is a new creature: old things are passed away; behold, all things are become new. 2 Corinthians 5:17

Covering Each Other's Weaknesses

Above all things have fervent charity among yourselves: for charity shall cover the multitude of sins. 1 Peter 4:8

Hatred stirreth up strifes: but love covereth all sins. Proverbs 10:12

And above all these things put on charity, which is the bond of perfectness. Colossians 3:14

Forbearing one another, and forgiving one another, if any man have a quarrel against any: even as Christ forgave you, so also do ye. Colossians 3:13

In marriage, we cover our spouse's weaknesses not to enable sin, but to protect their dignity while encouraging growth. - Gary Thomas

He that covereth a transgression seeketh love; but he that repeateth a matter separateth very friends. Proverbs 17:9

A friend loveth at all times, and a brother is born for adversity. Proverbs 17:17

Moving Forward Together

Brethren, I count not myself to have apprehended: but this one thing I do, forgetting those things which are behind, and reaching forth unto those things which are before, I press toward the mark for the prize of the high calling of God in Christ Jesus. Philippians 3:13-14

And we know that all things work together for good to them that love God, to them who are the called according to his purpose. Romans 8:28

For I know the thoughts that I think toward you, saith the Lord, thoughts of peace, and not of evil, to give you an expected end. Jeremiah 29:11

Can two walk together, except they be agreed? Amos 3:3

Moving forward together requires leaving the past behind and focusing on God's plan for your future as a couple. - Rick Warren

Therefore if any man be in Christ, he is a new creature: old things are passed away; behold, all things are become new. 2 Corinthians 5:17

Being confident of this very thing, that he which hath begun a good work in you will perform it until the day of Jesus Christ.
Philippians 1:6

Redemption in Marriage

And we know that all things work together for good to them that love God, to them who are the called according to his purpose.
Romans 8:28

But where sin abounded, grace did much more abound. Romans 5:20

And I will restore to you the years that the locust hath eaten, the cankerworm, and the caterpiller, and the palmerworm, my great army which I sent among you. Joel 2:25

To appoint unto them that mourn in Zion, to give unto them beauty for ashes, the oil of joy for mourning, the garment of praise for the spirit of heaviness. Isaiah 61:3

God can redeem any marriage, no matter how broken, and use the pain for His glory and your good. - Gary Thomas

Therefore if any man be in Christ, he is a new creature: old things are passed away; behold, all things are become new. 2 Corinthians 5:17

The thief cometh not, but for to steal, and to kill, and to destroy: I am come that they might have life, and that they might have it more abundantly. John 10:10

MARRIAGE CHALLENGES

Overcoming Marriage Problems

And we know that all things work together for good to them that love God, to them who are the called according to his purpose. Romans 8:28

These things I have spoken unto you, that in me ye might have peace. In the world ye shall have tribulation: but be of good cheer; I have overcome the world. John 16:33

For a just man falleth seven times, and riseth up again: but the wicked shall fall into mischief. Proverbs 24:16

Many are the afflictions of the righteous: but the Lord delivereth him out of them all. Psalms 34:19

Every marriage will face problems, but problems are opportunities for growth when approached with God's wisdom. - Gary Chapman
Submit yourselves therefore to God. Resist the devil, and he will flee from you. James 4:7

Be strong and of a good courage; be not afraid, neither be thou dismayed: for the Lord thy God is with thee whithersoever thou goest. Joshua 1:9

Surviving Difficult Seasons
To every thing there is a season, and a time to every purpose under the heaven. Ecclesiastes 3:1

Weeping may endure for a night, but joy cometh in the morning. Psalms 30:5

For his anger endureth but a moment; in his favour is life: weeping may endure for a night, but joy cometh in the morning. Psalms 30:5
The Lord is my shepherd; I shall not want. He maketh me to lie down in green pastures: he leadeth me beside the still waters. He restoreth my soul. Psalms 23:1-3

Difficult seasons in marriage are temporary. Hold onto each other and hold onto hope. - Dennis Rainey

And let us not be weary in well doing: for in due season we shall reap, if we faint not. Galatians 6:9

For I reckon that the sufferings of this present time are not worthy to be compared with the glory which shall be revealed in us. Romans 8:18

Financial Stress in Marriage

But my God shall supply all your need according to his riches in glory by Christ Jesus. Philippians 4:19

Therefore take no thought, saying, What shall we eat? or, What shall we drink? or, Wherewithal shall we be clothed? For your heavenly Father knoweth that ye have need of all these things. But seek ye first the kingdom of God, and his righteousness; and all these things shall be added unto you. Matthew 6:31-33

Owe no man any thing, but to love one another: for he that loveth another hath fulfilled the law. Romans 13:8

For the love of money is the root of all evil: which while some coveted after, they have erred from the faith, and pierced themselves through with many sorrows. 1 Timothy 6:10

Financial stress can destroy a marriage or strengthen it, depending on how the couple chooses to face it together. - Dave Ramsey

Be content with such things as ye have: for he hath said, I will never leave thee, nor forsake thee. Hebrews 13:5

And having food and raiment let us be therewith content. 1 Timothy 6:8

Dealing with In-Laws

Therefore shall a man leave his father and his mother, and shall cleave unto his wife: and they shall be one flesh. Genesis 2:24

Honour thy father and thy mother: that thy days may be long upon the land which the Lord thy God giveth thee. Exodus 20:12

And Ruth said, Intreat me not to leave thee, or to return from following after thee: for whither thou goest, I will go; and where thou lodgest, I will lodge: thy people shall be my people, and thy God my God. Ruth 1:16

Be ye kind one to another, tenderhearted, forgiving one another, even as God for Christ's sake hath forgiven you. Ephesians 4:32

Healthy boundaries with in-laws protect your marriage while still honoring your parents. - Henry Cloud

If it be possible, as much as lieth in you, live peaceably with all men. Romans 12:18

Let nothing be done through strife or vainglory; but in lowliness of mind let each esteem other better than themselves. Philippians 2:3

Infertility and Marriage

Lo, children are an heritage of the Lord: and the fruit of the womb is his reward. Psalms 127:3

And God remembered Rachel, and God hearkened to her, and opened her womb. Genesis 30:22

For this child I prayed; and the Lord hath given me my petition which I asked of him. 1 Samuel 1:27

And we know that all things work together for good to them that love God, to them who are the called according to his purpose. Romans 8:28

Infertility can bring a couple together in prayer and purpose, or it can drive them apart. Choose unity. - Gary Thomas

Wait on the Lord: be of good courage, and he shall strengthen thine heart: wait, I say, on the Lord. Psalms 27:14

For my thoughts are not your thoughts, neither are your ways my ways, saith the Lord. Isaiah 55:8

Parenting Challenges

Train up a child in the way he should go: and when he is old, he will not depart from it. Proverbs 22:6

And, ye fathers, provoke not your children to wrath: but bring them up in the nurture and admonition of the Lord. Ephesians 6:4

Children, obey your parents in the Lord: for this is right. Honour thy father and mother; which is the first commandment with promise. Ephesians 6:1-2

Chasten thy son while there is hope, and let not thy soul spare for his crying. Proverbs 19:18

Parenting challenges can strengthen a marriage when couples work as a unified team with consistent values. - James Dobson

The rod and reproof give wisdom: but a child left to himself bringeth his mother to shame. Proverbs 29:15

And these words, which I command thee this day, shall be in thine heart: And thou shalt teach them diligently unto thy children. Deuteronomy 6:6-7

Career and Marriage Balance

And whatsoever ye do in word or deed, do all in the name of the Lord Jesus, giving thanks to God and the Father by him. Colossians 3:17
But seek ye first the kingdom of God, and his righteousness; and all these things shall be added unto you. Matthew 6:33

And that ye study to be quiet, and to do your own business, and to work with your own hands, as we commanded you.
1 Thessalonians 4:11

In all labour there is profit: but the talk of the lips tendeth only to penury. Proverbs 14:23

Success at work means nothing if you fail at home. Your career should serve your marriage, not consume it. - Zig Ziglar

Better is little with the fear of the Lord than great treasure and trouble therewith. Proverbs 15:16

For what shall it profit a man, if he shall gain the whole world, and lose his own soul? Mark 8:36

Health Issues in Marriage

Is any sick among you? let him call for the elders of the church; and let them pray over him, anointing him with oil in the name of the Lord. James 5:14

But he was wounded for our transgressions, he was bruised for our iniquities: the chastisement of our peace was upon him; and with his stripes we are healed. Isaiah 53:5

Beloved, I wish above all things that thou mayest prosper and be in health, even as thy soul prospereth. 3 John 1:2

And Jesus went about all Galilee, teaching in their synagogues, and preaching the gospel of the kingdom, and healing all manner of sickness and all manner of disease among the people. Matthew 4:23

In sickness and in health means loving your spouse regardless of their physical condition. - Gary Chapman

In the day when I cried thou answeredst me, and strengthenedst me with strength in my soul. Psalms 138:3

He healeth the broken in heart, and bindeth up their wounds. Psalms 147:3

Depression and Marriage

The Lord is nigh unto them that are of a broken heart; and saveth such as be of a contrite spirit. Psalms 34:18

Why art thou cast down, O my soul? and why art thou disquieted in me? hope thou in God: for I shall yet praise him for the help of his countenance. Psalms 42:5

Come unto me, all ye that labour and are heavy laden, and I will give you rest. Matthew 11:28

He healeth the broken in heart, and bindeth up their wounds. Psalms 147:3

Depression affects the whole family. Love your spouse through their darkness while also seeking professional help. - Stephen Arterburn
Weeping may endure for a night, but joy cometh in the morning. Psalms 30:5

Cast thy burden upon the Lord, and he shall sustain thee: he shall never suffer the righteous to be moved. Psalms 55:22

Addiction Recovery in Marriage

Watch and pray, that ye enter not into temptation: the spirit indeed is willing, but the flesh is weak. Matthew 26:41

Submit yourselves therefore to God. Resist the devil, and he will flee from you. James 4:7

There hath no temptation taken you but such as is common to man: but God is faithful, who will not suffer you to be tempted above that ye are able; but will with the temptation also make a way to escape, that ye may be able to bear it. 1 Corinthians 10:13

If we confess our sins, he is faithful and just to forgive us our sins, and to cleanse us from all unrighteousness. 1 John 1:9

Addiction is a family disease that requires family healing. Recovery is possible with God's help and professional support. - John Baker

Therefore if any man be in Christ, he is a new creature: old things are passed away; behold, all things are become new. 2 Corinthians 5:17

And be not conformed to this world: but be ye transformed by the renewing of your mind. Romans 12:2

Rebuilding After Affair

If we confess our sins, he is faithful and just to forgive us our sins, and to cleanse us from all unrighteousness. 1 John 1:9

And I will restore to you the years that the locust hath eaten, the cankerworm, and the caterpiller, and the palmerworm, my great army which I sent among you. Joel 2:25

Brethren, if a man be overtaken in a fault, ye which are spiritual, restore such an one in the spirit of meekness; considering thyself, lest thou also be tempted. Galatians 6:1

Create in me a clean heart, O God; and renew a right spirit within me. Psalms 51:10

Rebuilding after an affair is possible but requires complete honesty, deep repentance, and time to rebuild trust. - Dave Carder

He hath not dealt with us after our sins; nor rewarded us according to our iniquities. Psalms 103:10

And their sins and iniquities will I remember no more. Hebrews 10:17

Pornography and Marriage

But I say unto you, That whosoever looketh on a woman to lust after her hath committed adultery with her already in his heart. Matthew 5:28

Marriage is honourable in all, and the bed undefiled: but whoremongers and adulterers God will judge. Hebrews 13:4

Flee fornication. Every sin that a man doeth is without the body; but he that committeth fornication sinneth against his own body. 1 Corinthians 6:18

Finally, brethren, whatsoever things are true, whatsoever things are honest, whatsoever things are just, whatsoever things are pure, whatsoever things are lovely, whatsoever things are of good report; if there be any virtue, and if there be any praise, think on these things. Philippians 4:8

Pornography destroys intimacy and trust in marriage. Freedom comes through accountability, transparency, and God's grace.
- Ted Roberts

Above all else, guard your heart, for everything you do flows from it. Proverbs 4:23

And have no fellowship with the unfruitful works of darkness, but rather reprove them. Ephesians 5:11

Anger Management

Be ye angry, and sin not: let not the sun go down upon your wrath. Ephesians 4:26

A soft answer turneth away wrath: but grievous words stir up anger. Proverbs 15:1

He that is slow to anger is better than the mighty; and he that ruleth his spirit than he that taketh a city. Proverbs 16:32

Wherefore, my beloved brethren, let every man be swift to hear, slow to speak, slow to wrath: For the wrath of man worketh not the righteousness of God. James 1:19-20

Anger is not always sin, but uncontrolled anger will destroy your marriage. Learn to manage it biblically. - Gary Chapman
A wrathful man stirreth up strife: but he that is slow to anger appeaseth strife. Proverbs 15:18

Cease from anger, and forsake wrath: fret not thyself in any wise to do evil. Psalms 37:8

Jealousy and Insecurity

A sound heart is the life of the flesh: but envy the rottenness of the bones. Proverbs 14:30

For where envying and strife is, there is confusion and every evil work. James 3:16

Charity suffereth long, and is kind; charity envieth not; charity vaunteth not itself, is not puffed up. 1 Corinthians 13:4

Let nothing be done through strife or vainglory; but in lowliness of mind let each esteem other better than themselves. Philippians 2:3

Jealousy is the fear of losing what you have; insecurity is the fear you're not worth keeping. Both destroy love. - John Gottman

Rest in the Lord, and wait patiently for him: fret not thyself because of him who prospereth in his way. Psalms 37:7

Set me as a seal upon thine heart, as a seal upon thine arm: for love is strong as death; jealousy is cruel as the grave.
Song of Solomon 8:6

Growing Apart

Can two walk together, except they be agreed? Amos 3:3

Two are better than one; because they have a good reward for their labour. For if they fall, the one will lift up his fellow: but woe to him that is alone when he falleth; for he hath not another to help him up. Ecclesiastes 4:9-10

Iron sharpeneth iron; so a man sharpeneth the countenance of his friend. Proverbs 27:17

And let us consider one another to provoke unto love and to good works. Hebrews 10:24

Growing apart happens when couples stop being intentional about growing together. - Gary Thomas

But grow in grace, and in the knowledge of our Lord and Saviour Jesus Christ. 2 Peter 3:18

Till we all come in the unity of the faith, and of the knowledge of the Son of God, unto a perfect man, unto the measure of the stature of the fulness of Christ. Ephesians 4:13

MID-LIFE MARRIAGE CRISIS

To every thing there is a season, and a time to every purpose under the heaven. Ecclesiastes 3:1

Remember ye not the former things, neither consider the things of old. Behold, I will do a new thing; now it shall spring forth; shall ye not know it? Isaiah 43:18-19

For I know the thoughts that I think toward you, saith the Lord, thoughts of peace, and not of evil, to give you an expected end. Jeremiah 29:11

And we know that all things work together for good to them that love God, to them who are the called according to his purpose. Romans 8:28

Mid-life crisis is often a search for meaning. Find your purpose together in God's plan for your marriage. - Tim Keller

Being confident of this very thing, that he which hath begun a good work in you will perform it until the day of Jesus Christ. Philippians 1:6

The path of the just is as the shining light, that shineth more and more unto the perfect day. Proverbs 4:18

Empty Nest Season

Lo, children are an heritage of the Lord: and the fruit of the womb is his reward. Psalms 127:3

To every thing there is a season, and a time to every purpose under the heaven. Ecclesiastes 3:1

Train up a child in the way he should go: and when he is old, he will not depart from it. Proverbs 22:6

For this cause shall a man leave his father and mother, and cleave to his wife; And they twain shall be one flesh: so then they are no more twain, but one flesh. Mark 10:7-8

The empty nest can be a new beginning for your marriage, not an ending. Rediscover each other. - Gary Chapman

Live joyfully with the wife whom thou lovest all the days of the life of thy vanity. Ecclesiastes 9:9

The glory of young men is their strength: and the beauty of old men is the grey head. Proverbs 20:29

Aging Together

The hoary head is a crown of glory, if it be found in the way of righteousness. Proverbs 16:31

Cast me not off in the time of old age; forsake me not when my strength faileth. Psalms 71:9

Even to your old age I am he; and even to hoar hairs will I carry you: I have made, and I will bear; even I will carry, and will deliver you. Isaiah 46:4

They shall still bring forth fruit in old age; they shall be fat and flourishing. Psalms 92:14

Growing old together is a privilege denied to many. Embrace each stage of life as a gift from God. - Billy Graham

The glory of young men is their strength: and the beauty of old men is the grey head. Proverbs 20:29

With the ancient is wisdom; and in length of days understanding. Job 12:12

Loss and Grief in Marriage

The Lord gave, and the Lord hath taken away; blessed be the name of the Lord. Job 1:21

Weeping may endure for a night, but joy cometh in the morning. Psalms 30:5

Blessed are they that mourn: for they shall be comforted. Matthew 5:4

Jesus wept. John 11:35

Grief shared is grief diminished. Walk through loss together, supporting each other through the pain. - Tim Keller

He healeth the broken in heart, and bindeth up their wounds. Psalms 147:3

And God shall wipe away all tears from their eyes; and there shall be no more death, neither sorrow, nor crying, neither shall there be any more pain: for the former things are passed away. Revelation 21:4

Spiritual Differences

Be ye not unequally yoked together with unbelievers: for what fellowship hath righteousness with unrighteousness? and what communion hath light with darkness? 2 Corinthians 6:14

Likewise, ye wives, be in subjection to your own husbands; that, if any obey not the word, they also may without the word be won by the conversation of the wives; While they behold your chaste conversation coupled with fear. 1 Peter 3:1-2

Can two walk together, except they be agreed? Amos 3:3

And if a woman hath a husband that believeth not, and he be pleased to dwell with her, let her not leave him. For the unbelieving husband is sanctified by the wife, and the unbelieving wife is sanctified by the husband. 1 Corinthians 7:13-14

When spouses are at different spiritual levels, patience, love, and a godly example speak louder than words. - Gary Thomas

But sanctify the Lord God in your hearts: and be ready always to give an answer to every man that asketh you a reason of the hope that is in you with meekness and fear. 1 Peter 3:15

Let your light so shine before men, that they may see your good works, and glorify your Father which is in heaven. Matthew 5:16

Cultural Differences

There is neither Jew nor Greek, there is neither bond nor free, there is neither male nor female: for ye are all one in Christ Jesus. Galatians 3:28

And hath made of one blood all nations of men for to dwell on all the face of the earth, and hath determined the times before appointed, and the bounds of their habitation. Acts 17:26

Be ye kind one to another, tenderhearted, forgiving one another, even as God for Christ's sake hath forgiven you. Ephesians 4:32

Let nothing be done through strife or vainglory; but in lowliness of mind let each esteem other better than themselves. Philippians 2:3

Cultural differences can enrich a marriage when approached with respect, understanding, and a willingness to learn. - Gary Chapman

If it be possible, as much as lieth in you, live peaceably with all men. Romans 12:18

Honour all men. Love the brotherhood. Fear God. Honour the king. 1 Peter 2:17

Blended Family Challenges

Train up a child in the way he should go: and when he is old, he will not depart from it. Proverbs 22:6

And, ye fathers, provoke not your children to wrath: but bring them up in the nurture and admonition of the Lord. Ephesians 6:4

Be ye kind one to another, tenderhearted, forgiving one another, even as God for Christ's sake hath forgiven you. Ephesians 4:32

And Ruth said, Intreat me not to leave thee, or to return from following after thee: for whither thou goest, I will go; and where thou lodgest, I will lodge: thy people shall be my people, and thy God my God. Ruth 1:16

Blending families requires patience, love, and time. Focus on building relationships, not forcing instant love. - Ron Deal
A friend loveth at all times, and a brother is born for adversity. Proverbs 17:17

Bear ye one another's burdens, and so fulfil the law of Christ. Galatians 6:2

Military Marriage

Be strong and of a good courage; be not afraid, neither be thou dismayed: for the Lord thy God is with thee whithersoever thou goest. Joshua 1:9

For he hath said, I will never leave thee, nor forsake thee. So that we may boldly say, The Lord is my helper, and I will not fear what man shall do unto me. Hebrews 13:5-6

Yea, though I walk through the valley of the shadow of death, I will fear no evil: for thou art with me; thy rod and thy staff they comfort me. Psalms 23:4

The Lord thy God in the midst of thee is mighty; he will save, he will rejoice over thee with joy; he will rest in his love, he will joy over thee with singing. Zephaniah 3:17

Military marriages face unique challenges of separation, danger, and frequent moves. Trust in God's protection and faithfulness.
- Marshéle Carter Waddell

I can do all things through Christ which strengtheneth me. Philippians 4:13

Wait on the Lord: be of good courage, and he shall strengthen thine heart: wait, I say, on the Lord. Psalms 27:14

Long-Distance Marriage

For he hath said, I will never leave thee, nor forsake thee. Hebrews 13:5

Yea, though I walk through the valley of the shadow of death, I will fear no evil: for thou art with me; thy rod and thy staff they comfort me. Psalms 23:4

And we know that all things work together for good to them that love God, to them who are the called according to his purpose. Romans 8:28

Two are better than one; because they have a good reward for their labour. Ecclesiastes 4:9

Distance tests love but doesn't have to destroy it. Communication, trust, and hope sustain long-distance marriages. - Gary Chapman

For I am persuaded, that neither death, nor life, nor angels, nor principalities, nor powers, nor things present, nor things to come, Nor height, nor depth, nor any other creature, shall be able to separate us from the love of God, which is in Christ Jesus our Lord. Romans 8:38-39

The Lord thy God in the midst of thee is mighty; he will save, he will rejoice over thee with joy. Zephaniah 3:17

Childless by Choice

Lo, children are an heritage of the Lord: and the fruit of the womb is his reward. Psalms 127:3

But I would have you without carefulness. He that is unmarried careth for the things that belong to the Lord, how he may please the Lord: But he that is married careth for the things that are of the world, how he may please his wife. 1 Corinthians 7:32-33

For there are some eunuchs, which were so born from their mother's womb: and there are some eunuchs, which were made eunuchs of men: and there be eunuchs, which have made themselves eunuchs for the kingdom of heaven's sake. He that is able to receive it, let him receive it. Matthew 19:12

But as God hath distributed to every man, as the Lord hath called every one, so let him walk. 1 Corinthians 7:17

Some couples are called to serve God without children. This choice can be godly when made prayerfully together. - Tim Keller

For my thoughts are not your thoughts, neither are your ways my ways, saith the Lord. Isaiah 55:8

And whatsoever ye do in word or deed, do all in the name of the Lord Jesus. Colossians 3:17

SPIRITUAL LIFE TOGETHER

Praying Together

Again I say unto you, That if two of you shall agree on earth as touching any thing that they shall ask, it shall be done for them of my Father which is in heaven. For where two or three are gathered together in my name, there am I in the midst of them.
Matthew 18:19-20

And they continued stedfastly in the apostles' doctrine and fellowship, and in breaking of bread, and in prayers. Acts 2:42

Pray without ceasing. 1 Thessalonians 5:17

Confess your faults one to another, and pray one for another, that ye may be healed. The effectual fervent prayer of a righteous man availeth much. James 5:16

The family that prays together stays together. Prayer unites hearts and invites God's presence into your marriage. - Patrick Morley

And it came to pass, that, as he was praying in a certain place, when he ceased, one of his disciples said unto him, Lord, teach us to pray, as John also taught his disciples. Luke 11:1

Call unto me, and I will answer thee, and shew thee great and mighty things, which thou knowest not. Jeremiah 33:3

Studying God's Word Together

All scripture is given by inspiration of God, and is profitable for doctrine, for reproof, for correction, for instruction in righteousness: That the man of God may be perfect, throughly furnished unto all good works. 2 Timothy 3:16-17

Study to shew thyself approved unto God, a workman that needeth not to be ashamed, rightly dividing the word of truth. 2 Timothy 2:15

Thy word is a lamp unto my feet, and a light unto my path. Psalms 119:105

And these words, which I command thee this day, shall be in thine heart: And thou shalt teach them diligently unto thy children, and shalt talk of them when thou sittest in thine house, and when thou walkest by the way, and when thou liest down, and when thou risest up. Deuteronomy 6:6-7

Couples who study God's Word together grow in wisdom and unity as they discover God's heart for their marriage. - Dennis Rainey

But his delight is in the law of the Lord; and in his law doth he meditate day and night. Psalms 1:2

The entrance of thy words giveth light; it giveth understanding unto the simple. Psalms 119:130

Worshiping as a Couple

O come, let us worship and bow down: let us kneel before the Lord our maker. Psalms 95:6

God is a Spirit: and they that worship him must worship him in spirit and in truth. John 4:24

By him therefore let us offer the sacrifice of praise to God continually, that is, the fruit of our lips giving thanks to his name. Hebrews 13:15

Speaking to yourselves in psalms and hymns and spiritual songs, singing and making melody in your heart to the Lord. Ephesians 5:19

Worship together draws you into God's presence and reminds you that your marriage is part of something greater than yourselves.
- Jack Hayford

But the hour cometh, and now is, when the true worshippers shall worship the Father in spirit and in truth: for the Father seeketh such to worship him. John 4:23

Let the word of Christ dwell in you richly in all wisdom; teaching and admonishing one another in psalms and hymns and spiritual songs, singing with grace in your hearts to the Lord. Colossians 3:16

Serving God Together

For we are his workmanship, created in Christ Jesus unto good works, which God hath before ordained that we should walk in them. Ephesians 2:10

And whatsoever ye do in word or deed, do all in the name of the Lord Jesus, giving thanks to God and the Father by him. Colossians 3:17

As every man hath received the gift, even so minister the same one to another, as good stewards of the manifold grace of God. 1 Peter 4:10

Two are better than one; because they have a good reward for their labour. Ecclesiastes 4:9

Serving God together multiplies your impact and unifies your purpose as a couple. - Gary Thomas

And let us not be weary in well doing: for in due season we shall reap, if we faint not. Galatians 6:9

For even the Son of man came not to be ministered unto, but to minister, and to give his life a ransom for many. Mark 10:45

Spiritual Growth in Marriage

But grow in grace, and in the knowledge of our Lord and Saviour Jesus Christ. To him be glory both now and for ever. Amen.
2 Peter 3:18

Iron sharpeneth iron; so a man sharpeneth the countenance of his friend. Proverbs 27:17

Till we all come in the unity of the faith, and of the knowledge of the Son of God, unto a perfect man, unto the measure of the stature of the fulness of Christ. Ephesians 4:13

And let us consider one another to provoke unto love and to good works. Hebrews 10:24

Marriage provides the perfect environment for spiritual growth as we learn to love sacrificially and grow in Christ-likeness. - Gary Thomas

But the path of the just is as the shining light, that shineth more and more unto the perfect day. Proverbs 4:18

Being confident of this very thing, that he which hath begun a good work in you will perform it until the day of Jesus Christ.
Philippians 1:6

Accountability in Marriage

Brethren, if a man be overtaken in a fault, ye which are spiritual, restore such an one in the spirit of meekness; considering thyself, lest thou also be tempted. Galatians 6:1

Confess your faults one to another, and pray one for another, that ye may be healed. The effectual fervent prayer of a righteous man availeth much. James 5:16

As iron sharpeneth iron; so a man sharpeneth the countenance of his friend. Proverbs 27:17

Faithful are the wounds of a friend; but the kisses of an enemy are deceitful. Proverbs 27:6

Your spouse can be your greatest accountability partner, helping you grow in holiness and obedience to God. - Gary Thomas

Two are better than one; because they have a good reward for their labour. For if they fall, the one will lift up his fellow: but woe to him that is alone when he falleth; for he hath not another to help him up. Ecclesiastes 4:9-10

Better is open rebuke than secret love. Proverbs 27:5

Fasting Together

And Jesus said unto them, Can the children of the bridechamber mourn, as long as the bridegroom is with them? but the days will come, when the bridegroom shall be taken from them, and then shall they fast. Matthew 9:15

Howbeit this kind goeth not out but by prayer and fasting. Matthew 17:21

Is not this the fast that I have chosen? to loose the bands of wickedness, to undo the heavy burdens, and to let the oppressed go free, and that ye break every yoke? Isaiah 58:6

Defraud ye not one the other, except it be with consent for a time, that ye may give yourselves to fasting and prayer; and come together again, that Satan tempt you not for your incontinency. 1 Corinthians 7:5

Fasting together as a couple can deepen your spiritual intimacy and strengthen your dependence on God. - Arthur Wallis

But thou, when thou fastest, anoint thine head, and wash thy face; That thou appear not unto men to fast, but unto thy Father which is in secret: and thy Father, which seeth in secret, shall reward thee openly. Matthew 6:17-18

Then I proclaimed a fast there, at the river of Ahava, that we might afflict ourselves before our God, to seek of him a right way for us, and for our little ones, and for all our substance. Ezra 8:21

Ministry as a Couple

For we are labourers together with God: ye are God's husbandry, ye are God's building. 1 Corinthians 3:9

And he gave some, apostles; and some, prophets; and some, evangelists; and some, pastors and teachers; For the perfecting of the saints, for the work of the ministry, for the edifying of the body of Christ. Ephesians 4:11-12

As every man hath received the gift, even so minister the same one to another, as good stewards of the manifold grace of God. 1 Peter 4:10

And whatsoever ye do in word or deed, do all in the name of the Lord Jesus, giving thanks to God and the Father by him. Colossians 3:17

Ministering together as a couple amplifies your effectiveness and demonstrates the unity that Christ desires for His church. - Dennis Rainey

Two are better than one; because they have a good reward for their labour. Ecclesiastes 4:9

For where two or three are gathered together in my name, there am I in the midst of them. Matthew 18:20

Evangelism in Marriage

Go ye therefore, and teach all nations, baptizing them in the name of the Father, and of the Son, and of the Holy Ghost. Matthew 28:19

But sanctify the Lord God in your hearts: and be ready always to give an answer to every man that asketh you a reason of the hope that is in you with meekness and fear. 1 Peter 3:15

Let your light so shine before men, that they may see your good works, and glorify your Father which is in heaven. Matthew 5:16

Likewise, ye wives, be in subjection to your own husbands; that, if any obey not the word, they also may without the word be won by the conversation of the wives. 1 Peter 3:1

A godly marriage is one of the most powerful evangelistic tools in existence. - Gary Thomas

And Jesus said unto them, Come ye after me, and I will make you to become fishers of men. Mark 1:17

By this shall all men know that ye are my disciples, if ye have love one to another. John 13:35

Discipleship in Marriage

And he said to them all, If any man will come after me, let him deny himself, and take up his cross daily, and follow me. Luke 9:23

Iron sharpeneth iron; so a man sharpeneth the countenance of his friend. Proverbs 27:17

And the things that thou hast heard of me among many witnesses, the same commit thou to faithful men, who shall be able to teach others also. 2 Timothy 2:2

Teaching them to observe all things whatsoever I have commanded you: and, lo, I am with you alway, even unto the end of the world. Amen. Matthew 28:20

In marriage, you have the unique opportunity to disciple and be discipled by your closest earthly companion. - Gary Thomas

Till we all come in the unity of the faith, and of the knowledge of the Son of God, unto a perfect man, unto the measure of the stature of the fulness of Christ. Ephesians 4:13

But grow in grace, and in the knowledge of our Lord and Saviour Jesus Christ. 2 Peter 3:18

Church Life and Marriage

Not forsaking the assembling of ourselves together, as the manner of some is; but exhorting one another: and so much the more, as ye see the day approaching. Hebrews 10:25

And let us consider one another to provoke unto love and to good works. Hebrews 10:24

For as the body is one, and hath many members, and all the members of that one body, being many, are one body: so also is Christ. 1 Corinthians 12:12

And they continued stedfastly in the apostles' doctrine and fellowship, and in breaking of bread, and in prayers. Acts 2:42

Active participation in church life strengthens your marriage and provides community support for your relationship. - Dennis Rainey

Iron sharpeneth iron; so a man sharpeneth the countenance of his friend. Proverbs 27:17

Bear ye one another's burdens, and so fulfil the law of Christ. Galatians 6:2

Giving as a Couple

Upon the first day of the week let every one of you lay by him in store, as God hath prospered him, that there be no gatherings when I come. 1 Corinthians 16:2

Every man according as he purposeth in his heart, so let him give; not grudgingly, or of necessity: for God loveth a cheerful giver. 2 Corinthians 9:7

Give, and it shall be given unto you; good measure, pressed down, and shaken together, and running over, shall men give into your bosom. For with the same measure that ye mete withal it shall be measured to you again. Luke 6:38

Honour the Lord with thy substance, and with the firstfruits of all thine increase: So shall thy barns be filled with plenty, and thy presses shall burst out with new wine. Proverbs 3:9-10

Generous giving as a couple demonstrates trust in God's provision and unity in your values. - Dave Ramsey

Bring ye all the tithes into the storehouse, that there may be meat in mine house, and prove me now herewith, saith the Lord of hosts, if I will not open you the windows of heaven, and pour you out a blessing, that there shall not be room enough to receive it. Malachi 3:10

But this I say, He which soweth sparingly shall reap also sparingly; and he which soweth bountifully shall reap also bountifully.
2 Corinthians 9:6

Spiritual Warfare in Marriage

Finally, my brethren, be strong in the Lord, and in the power of his might. Put on the whole armour of God, that ye may be able to stand against the wiles of the devil. For we wrestle not against flesh and blood, but against principalities, against powers, against the rulers of the darkness of this world, against spiritual wickedness in high places. Ephesians 6:10-12

Submit yourselves therefore to God. Resist the devil, and he will flee from you. James 4:7

Be sober, be vigilant; because your adversary the devil, as a roaring lion, walketh about, seeking whom he may devour: Whom resist stedfast in the faith, knowing that the same afflictions are accomplished in your brethren that are in the world. 1 Peter 5:8-9

And they overcame him by the blood of the Lamb, and by the word of their testimony; and they loved not their lives unto the death. Revelation 12:11

Marriage is under spiritual attack. Fight together, not against each other, recognizing your real enemy. - Neil Anderson

Above all, taking the shield of faith, wherewith ye shall be able to quench all the fiery darts of the wicked. Ephesians 6:16

The weapons of our warfare are not carnal, but mighty through God to the pulling down of strong holds. 2 Corinthians 10:4

Seeking God's Will Together

Trust in the Lord with all thine heart; and lean not unto thine own understanding. In all thy ways acknowledge him, and he shall direct thy paths. Proverbs 3:5-6

And be not conformed to this world: but be ye transformed by the renewing of your mind, that ye may prove what is that good, and acceptable, and perfect, will of God. Romans 12:2

For I know the thoughts that I think toward you, saith the Lord, thoughts of peace, and not of evil, to give you an expected end. Jeremiah 29:11

Can two walk together, except they be agreed? Amos 3:3
Seeking God's will together ensures your marriage moves in the direction God intends. - Gary Thomas

If any of you lack wisdom, let him ask of God, that giveth to all men liberally, and upbraideth not; and it shall be given him. James 1:5

Commit thy way unto the Lord; trust also in him; and he shall bring it to pass. Psalms 37:5

Building a Legacy

The just man walketh in his integrity: his children are blessed after him. Proverbs 20:7

One generation shall praise thy works to another, and shall declare thy mighty acts. Psalms 145:4

And he shall turn the heart of the fathers to the children, and the heart of the children to their fathers, lest I come and smite the earth with a curse. Malachi 4:6

A good man leaveth an inheritance to his children's children: and the wealth of the sinner is laid up for the just. Proverbs 13:22

And these words, which I command thee this day, shall be in thine heart: And thou shalt teach them diligently unto thy children, and shalt talk of them when thou sittest in thine house, and when thou walkest by the way, and when thou liest down, and when thou risest up. Deuteronomy 6:6-7

Your marriage legacy is not just what you leave behind, but what you live out day by day. - Dennis Rainey

The memory of the just is blessed: but the name of the wicked shall rot. Proverbs 10:7

PRACTICAL MARRIAGE LIFE

Daily Rhythms in Marriage

To every thing there is a season, and a time to every purpose under the heaven. Ecclesiastes 3:1

And that ye study to be quiet, and to do your own business, and to work with your own hands, as we commanded you.
1 Thessalonians 4:11

But all things must be done decently and in order.
1 Corinthians 14:40

Establishing the work of our hands upon us; yea, the work of our hands establish thou it. Psalms 90:17

Healthy daily rhythms create stability and connection in marriage. Make time for each other every day. - Gary Chapman

This is the day which the Lord hath made; we will rejoice and be glad in it. Psalms 118:24

The steps of a good man are ordered by the Lord: and he delighteth in his way. Psalms 37:23

Creating Traditions

One generation shall praise thy works to another, and shall declare thy mighty acts. Psalms 145:4

And it shall be when thy son asketh thee in time to come, saying, What mean these stones? Then ye shall answer them.
Joshua 4:21-22

A good man leaveth an inheritance to his children's children.
Proverbs 13:22

And these words, which I command thee this day, shall be in thine heart: And thou shalt teach them diligently unto thy children, and shalt talk of them when thou sittest in thine house.
Deuteronomy 6:6-7

Remember ye the law of Moses my servant, which I commanded unto him in Horeb for all Israel, with the statutes and judgments.
Malachi 4:4

Traditions create shared memories and strengthen family bonds across generations. - Dennis Rainey

Celebrating Milestones

This is the day which the Lord hath made; we will rejoice and be glad in it. Psalms 118:24

A time to weep, and a time to laugh; a time to mourn, and a time to dance. Ecclesiastes 3:4

And Mordecai wrote these things, and sent letters unto all the Jews that were in all the provinces of the king Ahasuerus, both nigh and far, To stablish this among them, that they should keep the fourteenth day of the month Adar, and the fifteenth day of the same, yearly, As the days wherein the Jews rested from their enemies, and the month which was turned unto them from sorrow to joy, and from mourning into a good day: that they should make them days of feasting and joy. Esther 9:20-22

Let us be glad and rejoice, and give honour to him: for the marriage of the Lamb is come, and his wife hath made herself ready.
Revelation 19:7

Celebrating milestones acknowledges God's faithfulness and creates joyful memories in your marriage. - Gary Chapman

In every thing give thanks: for this is the will of God in Christ Jesus concerning you. 1 Thessalonians 5:18

Rejoice with them that do rejoice, and weep with them that weep. Romans 12:15

Date Night Importance

Live joyfully with the wife whom thou lovest all the days of the life of thy vanity, which he hath given thee under the sun, all the days of thy vanity: for that is thy portion in this life, and in thy labour which thou takest under the sun. Ecclesiastes 9:9

Let thy fountain be blessed: and rejoice with the wife of thy youth. Proverbs 5:18

My beloved spake, and said unto me, Rise up, my love, my fair one, and come away. Song of Solomon 2:10

Come with me from Lebanon, my spouse, with me from Lebanon: look from the top of Amana, from the top of Shenir and Hermon, from the lions' dens, from the mountains of the leopards. Song of Solomon 4:8

Regular date nights keep romance alive and provide dedicated time for connection without distractions. - Gary Chapman

A time to embrace, and a time to refrain from embracing. Ecclesiastes 3:5

I am my beloved's, and my beloved is mine. Song of Solomon 6:3

Vacation and Rest

And he said unto them, Come ye yourselves apart into a desert place, and rest a while: for there were many coming and going, and they had no leisure so much as to eat. Mark 6:31

It is vain for you to rise up early, to sit up late, to eat the bread of sorrows: for so he giveth his beloved sleep. Psalms 127:2

And on the seventh day God ended his work which he had made; and he rested on the seventh day from all his work which he had made. Genesis 2:2

Come unto me, all ye that labour and are heavy laden, and I will give you rest. Matthew 11:28

Regular rest and vacation times strengthen marriages by providing opportunities for renewal and deeper connection. - Gary Thomas

Six days thou shalt work, but on the seventh day thou shalt rest: in earing time and in harvest thou shalt rest. Exodus 34:21

Remember the sabbath day, to keep it holy. Exodus 20:8

Hospitality in Marriage

Be not forgetful to entertain strangers: for thereby some have entertained angels unawares. Hebrews 13:2

Use hospitality one to another without grudging. 1 Peter 4:9

Given to hospitality. Romans 12:13

But a lover of hospitality, a lover of good men, sober, just, holy, temperate. Titus 1:8

Hospitality opens your home and heart to others, strengthening your marriage through shared service. - Karen Mains

And into whatsoever house ye enter, first say, Peace be to this house. Luke 10:5

Distributing to the necessity of saints; given to hospitality. Romans 12:13

Managing Household Duties

She looketh well to the ways of her household, and eateth not the bread of idleness. Proverbs 31:27

And that ye study to be quiet, and to do your own business, and to work with your own hands, as we commanded you.
1 Thessalonians 4:11

Through wisdom is an house builded; and by understanding it is established: And by knowledge shall the chambers be filled with all precious and pleasant riches. Proverbs 24:3-4

In all labour there is profit: but the talk of the lips tendeth only to penury. Proverbs 14:23

Sharing household duties fairly strengthens partnership and prevents resentment in marriage. - Gary Chapman

And whatsoever ye do in word or deed, do all in the name of the Lord Jesus, giving thanks to God and the Father by him. Colossians 3:17

Let all things be done decently and in order. 1 Corinthians 14:40

Financial Partnership

Owe no man any thing, but to love one another: for he that loveth another hath fulfilled the law. Romans 13:8

For which of you, intending to build a tower, sitteth not down first, and counteth the cost, whether he have sufficient to finish it? Luke 14:28

Be thou diligent to know the state of thy flocks, and look well to thy herds. For riches are not for ever: and doth the crown endure to every generation? Proverbs 27:23-24

In the house of the righteous is much treasure: but in the revenues of the wicked is trouble. Proverbs 15:6

Financial partnership in marriage requires transparency, shared goals, and wise stewardship of God's resources. - Dave Ramsey

But my God shall supply all your need according to his riches in glory by Christ Jesus. Philippians 4:19

Honour the Lord with thy substance, and with the firstfruits of all thine increase. Proverbs 3:9

Decision Making Together

Where no counsel is, the people fall: but in the multitude of counsellors there is safety. Proverbs 11:14

Two are better than one; because they have a good reward for their labour. Ecclesiastes 4:9

Can two walk together, except they be agreed? Amos 3:3

Every purpose is established by counsel: and with good advice make war. Proverbs 20:18

Good decision making in marriage requires communication, prayer, and mutual respect for each other's wisdom. - Gary Thomas

Trust in the Lord with all thine heart; and lean not unto thine own understanding. In all thy ways acknowledge him, and he shall direct thy paths. Proverbs 3:5-6

If any of you lack wisdom, let him ask of God, that giveth to all men liberally, and upbraideth not; and it shall be given him. James 1:5

Goal Setting as a Couple

Where there is no vision, the people perish: but he that keepeth the law, happy is he. Proverbs 29:18

For I know the thoughts that I think toward you, saith the Lord, thoughts of peace, and not of evil, to give you an expected end. Jeremiah 29:11

A man's heart deviseth his way: but the Lord directeth his steps. Proverbs 16:9

Commit thy works unto the Lord, and thy thoughts shall be established. Proverbs 16:3

Setting goals together creates unity of purpose and helps couples work toward a shared future. - Gary Chapman

But seek ye first the kingdom of God, and his righteousness; and all these things shall be added unto you. Matthew 6:33

In all thy ways acknowledge him, and he shall direct thy paths.
Proverbs 3:6

Time Management

To every thing there is a season, and a time to every purpose under the heaven. Ecclesiastes 3:1

See then that ye walk circumspectly, not as fools, but as wise, Redeeming the time, because the days are evil. Ephesians 5:15-16

So teach us to number our days, that we may apply our hearts unto wisdom. Psalms 90:12

The steps of a good man are ordered by the Lord: and he delighteth in his way. Psalms 37:23

Good time management in marriage ensures you have time for what matters most - God, each other, and family. - Stephen Covey
But all things must be done decently and in order.
1 Corinthians 14:40

For which of you, intending to build a tower, sitteth not down first, and counteth the cost, whether he have sufficient to finish it?
Luke 14:28

Building Friendships as a Couple

Iron sharpeneth iron; so a man sharpeneth the countenance of his friend. Proverbs 27:17

A friend loveth at all times, and a brother is born for adversity.
Proverbs 17:17

As iron sharpeneth iron; so a man sharpeneth the countenance of his friend. Proverbs 27:17

Bear ye one another's burdens, and so fulfil the law of Christ. Galatians 6:2

Building friendships as a couple provides community support and models godly relationships for others. - Dave and Claudia Arp

Two are better than one; because they have a good reward for their labour. Ecclesiastes 4:9

Not forsaking the assembling of ourselves together, as the manner of some is; but exhorting one another. Hebrews 10:25

Social Life in Marriage

Be ye kind one to another, tenderhearted, forgiving one another, even as God for Christ's sake hath forgiven you. Ephesians 4:32

Let nothing be done through strife or vainglory; but in lowliness of mind let each esteem other better than themselves. Philippians 2:3

If it be possible, as much as lieth in you, live peaceably with all men. Romans 12:18

Use hospitality one to another without grudging. 1 Peter 4:9

A healthy social life enriches marriage through meaningful relationships and shared experiences with others. - Gary Chapman

Iron sharpeneth iron; so a man sharpeneth the countenance of his friend. Proverbs 27:17

And let us consider one another to provoke unto love and to good works. Hebrews 10:24

Technology and Marriage

Finally, brethren, whatsoever things are true, whatsoever things are honest, whatsoever things are just, whatsoever things are pure, whatsoever things are lovely, whatsoever things are of good report; if there be any virtue, and if there be any praise, think on these things. Philippians 4:8

Above all else, guard your heart, for everything you do flows from it. Proverbs 4:23

All things are lawful unto me, but all things are not expedient: all things are lawful for me, but I will not be brought under the power of any. 1 Corinthians 6:12

Redeeming the time, because the days are evil. Ephesians 5:16

Technology should serve your marriage, not rule it. Set boundaries to protect your time and attention for each other. - Gary Chapman

Let no corrupt communication proceed out of your mouth, but that which is good to the use of edifying, that it may minister grace unto the hearers. Ephesians 4:29

Be sober, be vigilant; because your adversary the devil, as a roaring lion, walketh about, seeking whom he may devour. 1 Peter 5:8

Work-Life Balance

And that ye study to be quiet, and to do your own business, and to work with your own hands, as we commanded you; That ye may walk honestly toward them that are without, and that ye may have lack of nothing. 1 Thessalonians 4:11-12

Six days thou shalt work, but on the seventh day thou shalt rest: in earing time and in harvest thou shalt rest. Exodus 34:21

It is vain for you to rise up early, to sit up late, to eat the bread of sorrows: for so he giveth his beloved sleep. Psalms 127:2

But seek ye first the kingdom of God, and his righteousness; and all these things shall be added unto you. Matthew 6:33

Work should provide for your family, not consume it. Balance is essential for a healthy marriage. - Gary Thomas

Better is little with the fear of the Lord than great treasure and trouble therewith. Proverbs 15:16

For what shall it profit a man, if he shall gain the whole world, and lose his own soul? Mark 8:36

Retirement Planning

Be thou diligent to know the state of thy flocks, and look well to thy herds. For riches are not for ever: and doth the crown endure to every generation? Proverbs 27:23-24

A good man leaveth an inheritance to his children's children: and the wealth of the sinner is laid up for the just. Proverbs 13:22

In the house of the righteous is much treasure: but in the revenues of the wicked is trouble. Proverbs 15:6

For which of you, intending to build a tower, sitteth not down first, and counteth the cost, whether he have sufficient to finish it? Luke 14:28

Planning for retirement together ensures you can serve God and enjoy your later years without financial stress. - Dave Ramsey

Commit thy works unto the Lord, and thy thoughts shall be established. Proverbs 16:3

Trust in the Lord with all thine heart; and lean not unto thine own understanding. Proverbs 3:5

Health and Wellness Together

Beloved, I wish above all things that thou mayest prosper and be in health, even as thy soul prospereth. 3 John 1:2

What? know ye not that your body is the temple of the Holy Ghost which is in you, which ye have of God, and ye are not your own? For ye are bought with a price: therefore glorify God in your body, and in your spirit, which are God's. 1 Corinthians 6:19-20

And be not conformed to this world: but be ye transformed by the renewing of your mind, that ye may prove what is that good, and acceptable, and perfect, will of God. Romans 12:2

Whether therefore ye eat, or drink, or whatsoever ye do, do all to the glory of God. 1 Corinthians 10:31

Taking care of your health together shows love for each other and stewardship of the bodies God has given you. - Gary Thomas

In all labour there is profit: but the talk of the lips tendeth only to penury. Proverbs 14:23

She girdeth her loins with strength, and strengtheneth her arms. Proverbs 31:17

Recreation and Fun

A merry heart doeth good like a medicine: but a broken spirit drieth the bones. Proverbs 17:22

A time to weep, and a time to laugh; a time to mourn, and a time to dance. Ecclesiastes 3:4

Live joyfully with the wife whom thou lovest all the days of the life of thy vanity, which he hath given thee under the sun, all the days of thy vanity: for that is thy portion in this life, and in thy labour which thou takest under the sun. Ecclesiastes 9:9

The light of the eyes rejoiceth the heart: and a good report maketh the bones fat. Proverbs 15:30

Fun and recreation in marriage create joy, reduce stress, and strengthen your emotional bond. - Gary Chapman

A merry heart maketh a cheerful countenance: but by sorrow of the heart the spirit is broken. Proverbs 15:13

Then he said unto them, Go your way, eat the fat, and drink the sweet, and send portions unto them for whom nothing is prepared: for this day is holy unto our Lord: neither be ye sorry; for the joy of the Lord is your strength. Nehemiah 8:10

Learning Together

The heart of the prudent getteth knowledge; and the ear of the wise seeketh knowledge. Proverbs 18:15

Study to shew thyself approved unto God, a workman that needeth not to be ashamed, rightly dividing the word of truth. 2 Timothy 2:15

Iron sharpeneth iron; so a man sharpeneth the countenance of his friend. Proverbs 27:17

And beside this, giving all diligence, add to your faith virtue; and to virtue knowledge. 2 Peter 1:5

Learning together keeps your marriage fresh and helps you grow intellectually and spiritually as a team. - Gary Thomas

The simple believeth every word: but the prudent man looketh well to his going. Proverbs 14:15

Apply thine heart unto instruction, and thine ears to the words of knowledge. Proverbs 23:12

Supporting Each Other's Growth

Let nothing be done through strife or vainglory; but in lowliness of mind let each esteem other better than themselves. Look not every man on his own things, but every man also on the things of others. Philippians 2:3-4

Iron sharpeneth iron; so a man sharpeneth the countenance of his friend. Proverbs 27:17

And let us consider one another to provoke unto love and to good works. Hebrews 10:24

Bear ye one another's burdens, and so fulfil the law of Christ. Galatians 6:2

Supporting each other's growth means helping your spouse become all that God has called them to be. - Gary Thomas

As every man hath received the gift, even so minister the same one to another, as good stewards of the manifold grace of God. 1 Peter 4:10

Two are better than one; because they have a good reward for their labour. Ecclesiastes 4:9

Creating a Peaceful Home

Better is a dry morsel, and quietness therewith, than an house full of sacrifices with strife. Proverbs 17:1

Through wisdom is an house builded; and by understanding it is established: And by knowledge shall the chambers be filled with all precious and pleasant riches. Proverbs 24:3-4

It is better to dwell in the corner of the housetop, than with a brawling woman and in a wide house. Proverbs 25:24

As for me and my house, we will serve the Lord. Joshua 24:15

A peaceful home is a sanctuary where family members can rest, grow, and find refuge from the world. - Emilie Barnes

Blessed are the peacemakers: for they shall be called the children of God. Matthew 5:9

Let the peace of God rule in your hearts, to the which also ye are called in one body; and be ye thankful. Colossians 3:15

Organizing Your Life Together

Let all things be done decently and in order. 1 Corinthians 14:40

For which of you, intending to build a tower, sitteth not down first, and counteth the cost, whether he have sufficient to finish it? Luke 14:28

The preparations of the heart in man, and the answer of the tongue, is from the Lord. Proverbs 16:1

A man's heart deviseth his way: but the Lord directeth his steps. Proverbs 16:9

Organization in marriage reduces stress and creates space for what matters most - your relationship with God and each other.
- Gary Chapman

But all things must be done decently and in order.
1 Corinthians 14:40

Commit thy works unto the Lord, and thy thoughts shall be established. Proverbs 16:3

Travel and Adventure

And Jesus said unto them, Come ye yourselves apart into a desert place, and rest a while: for there were many coming and going, and they had no leisure so much as to eat. Mark 6:31

Every place that the sole of your foot shall tread upon, that have I given unto you, as I said unto Moses. Joshua 1:3

And they went forth, and preached every where, the Lord working with them, and confirming the word with signs following. Amen. Mark 16:20

And he said unto them, Go ye into all the world, and preach the gospel to every creature. Mark 16:15

Travel and adventure together create shared memories and opportunities to see God's creation and goodness. - Gary Chapman

The earth is the Lord's, and the fulness thereof; the world, and they that dwell therein. Psalms 24:1

When thou goest, thy steps shall not be straitened; and when thou runnest, thou shalt not stumble. Proverbs 4:12

Seasonal Adjustments

To every thing there is a season, and a time to every purpose under the heaven. Ecclesiastes 3:1

While the earth remaineth, seedtime and harvest, and cold and heat, and summer and winter, and day and night shall not cease. Genesis 8:22

He hath made every thing beautiful in his time: also he hath set the world in their heart, so that no man can find out the work that God maketh from the beginning to the end. Ecclesiastes 3:11

For he saith, I have heard thee in a time accepted, and in the day of salvation have I succoured thee: behold, now is the accepted time; behold, now is the day of salvation. 2 Corinthians 6:2

Marriage goes through seasons. Embrace each one and adjust your expectations and priorities accordingly. - Gary Thomas

And let us not be weary in well doing: for in due season we shall reap, if we faint not. Galatians 6:9

The Lord is good unto them that wait for him, to the soul that seeketh him. Lamentations 3:25

Daily Encouragement

Therefore comfort yourselves together, and edify one another, even as also ye do. 1 Thessalonians 5:11

Pleasant words are as an honeycomb, sweet to the soul, and health to the bones. Proverbs 16:24

A word fitly spoken is like apples of gold in pictures of silver. Proverbs 25:11

And let us consider one another to provoke unto love and to good works. Hebrews 10:24

Daily encouragement is like water to a plant - essential for growth and flourishing in marriage. - Gary Chapman

Let no corrupt communication proceed out of your mouth, but that which is good to the use of edifying, that it may minister grace unto the hearers. Ephesians 4:29

Wherefore lift up the hands which hang down, and the feeble knees. Hebrews 12:12

MARRIAGE PROTECTION AND WISDOM

Setting Boundaries

Above all else, guard your heart, for everything you do flows from it. Proverbs 4:23

Watch and pray, that ye enter not into temptation: the spirit indeed is willing, but the flesh is weak. Matthew 26:41

Flee fornication. Every sin that a man doeth is without the body; but he that committeth fornication sinneth against his own body. 1 Corinthians 6:18

Be sober, be vigilant; because your adversary the devil, as a roaring lion, walketh about, seeking whom he may devour. 1 Peter 5:8

Healthy boundaries protect your marriage from external threats and internal weaknesses. - Henry Cloud

Can a man take fire in his bosom, and his clothes not be burned? Can one go upon hot coals, and his feet not be burned? Proverbs 6:27-28

Submit yourselves therefore to God. Resist the devil, and he will flee from you. James 4:7

Avoiding Temptation

There hath no temptation taken you but such as is common to man: but God is faithful, who will not suffer you to be tempted above that ye are able; but will with the temptation also make a way to escape, that ye may be able to bear it. 1 Corinthians 10:13

Watch and pray, that ye enter not into temptation: the spirit indeed is willing, but the flesh is weak. Matthew 26:41

But every man is tempted, when he is drawn away of his own lust, and enticed. Then when lust hath conceived, it bringeth forth sin: and sin, when it is finished, bringeth forth death. James 1:14-15

Flee also youthful lusts: but follow righteousness, faith, charity, peace, with them that call on the Lord out of a pure heart.
2 Timothy 2:22

The best way to handle temptation is to avoid it entirely. Build safeguards around your marriage. - Billy Graham

Thy word have I hid in mine heart, that I might not sin against thee. Psalms 119:11

Lead us not into temptation, but deliver us from evil: For thine is the kingdom, and the power, and the glory, for ever. Amen. Matthew 6:13

Guarding Your Heart

Keep thy heart with all diligence; for out of it are the issues of life. Proverbs 4:23

A good man out of the good treasure of the heart bringeth forth good things: and an evil man out of the evil treasure bringeth forth evil things. Matthew 12:35

Finally, brethren, whatsoever things are true, whatsoever things are honest, whatsoever things are just, whatsoever things are pure, whatsoever things are lovely, whatsoever things are of good report; if there be any virtue, and if there be any praise, think on these things. Philippians 4:8

Set your affection on things above, not on things on the earth. Colossians 3:2

Your heart is the wellspring of your marriage. Guard it carefully from influences that would poison your love. - Gary Thomas

The heart is deceitful above all things, and desperately wicked: who can know it? Jeremiah 17:9

Create in me a clean heart, O God; and renew a right spirit within me. Psalms 51:10

Wisdom in Marriage

If any of you lack wisdom, let him ask of God, that giveth to all men liberally, and upbraideth not; and it shall be given him. James 1:5

The fear of the Lord is the beginning of wisdom: and the knowledge of the holy is understanding. Proverbs 9:10

Through wisdom is an house builded; and by understanding it is established: And by knowledge shall the chambers be filled with all precious and pleasant riches. Proverbs 24:3-4

Where no counsel is, the people fall: but in the multitude of counsellors there is safety. Proverbs 11:14

Wisdom is the principal thing; therefore get wisdom: and with all thy getting get understanding. Proverbs 4:7

Happy is the man that findeth wisdom, and the man that getteth understanding. For the merchandise of it is better than the merchandise of silver, and the gain thereof than fine gold. Proverbs 3:13-14

A wise man will hear, and will increase learning; and a man of understanding shall attain unto wise counsels. Proverbs 1:5

Discernment in Relationships

Beloved, believe not every spirit, but try the spirits whether they are of God: because many false prophets are gone out into the world. 1 John 4:1

The simple believeth every word: but the prudent man looketh well to his going. Proverbs 14:15

But strong meat belongeth to them that are of full age, even those who by reason of use have their senses exercised to discern both good and evil. Hebrews 5:14

Prove all things; hold fast that which is good. 1 Thessalonians 5:21

Discernment helps you choose friends and influences that strengthen rather than weaken your marriage. - Gary Thomas

A righteous man is cautious in friendship, but the way of the wicked leads them astray. Proverbs 12:26

Iron sharpeneth iron; so a man sharpeneth the countenance of his friend. Proverbs 27:17

Avoiding Divorce

What therefore God hath joined together, let not man put asunder. Mark 10:9

For the Lord, the God of Israel, saith that he hateth putting away: for one covereth violence with his garment, saith the Lord of hosts: therefore take heed to your spirit, that ye deal not treacherously. Malachi 2:16

And unto the married I command, yet not I, but the Lord, Let not the wife depart from her husband: But and if she depart, let her remain unmarried, or be reconciled to her husband: and let not the husband put away his wife. 1 Corinthians 7:10-11

But from the beginning of the creation God made them male and female. For this cause shall a man leave his father and mother, and cleave to his wife; And they twain shall be one flesh: so then they are no more twain, but one flesh. Mark 10:6-8

Divorce should be the last resort, not the first option when problems arise in marriage. - Gary Chapman

Yet ye say, Wherefore? Because the Lord hath been witness between thee and the wife of thy youth, against whom thou hast dealt treacherously: yet is she thy companion, and the wife of thy covenant. Malachi 2:14

And I say unto you, Whosoever shall put away his wife, except it be for fornication, and shall marry another, committeth adultery: and whoso marrieth her which is put away doth commit adultery. Matthew 19:9

Getting Godly Counsel

Where no counsel is, the people fall: but in the multitude of counsellors there is safety. Proverbs 11:14

The way of a fool is right in his own eyes: but he that hearkeneth unto counsel is wise. Proverbs 12:15

Every purpose is established by counsel: and with good advice make war. Proverbs 20:18

Without counsel purposes are disappointed: but in the multitude of counsellors they are established. Proverbs 15:22

Seeking godly counsel can prevent many marriage problems and provide wisdom for difficult situations. - Gary Thomas

Hear counsel, and receive instruction, that thou mayest be wise in thy latter end. Proverbs 19:20

The simple believeth every word: but the prudent man looketh well to his going. Proverbs 14:15

Learning from Other Couples

Remember them which have the rule over you, who have spoken unto you the word of God: whose faith follow, considering the end of their conversation. Hebrews 13:7

Wherefore I beseech you, be ye followers of me. 1 Corinthians 4:16
Those things, which ye have both learned, and received, and heard, and seen in me, do: and the God of peace shall be with you. Philippians 4:9

One generation shall praise thy works to another, and shall declare thy mighty acts. Psalms 145:4

Learning from couples who have strong marriages provides wisdom and inspiration for your own relationship. - Dennis Rainey
Iron sharpeneth iron; so a man sharpeneth the countenance of his friend. Proverbs 27:17

Be ye followers of me, even as I also am of Christ. 1 Corinthians 11:1

Marriage Mentoring

And the things that thou hast heard of me among many witnesses, the same commit thou to faithful men, who shall be able to teach others also. 2 Timothy 2:2

The aged women likewise, that they be in behaviour as becometh holiness, not false accusers, not given to much wine, teachers of good things; That they may teach the young women to be sober, to love their husbands, to love their children. Titus 2:3-4

Iron sharpeneth iron; so a man sharpeneth the countenance of his friend. Proverbs 27:17

And let us consider one another to provoke unto love and to good works. Hebrews 10:24

Both receiving and giving marriage mentoring strengthens marriages and builds the next generation.
 - Dennis and Barbara Rainey

The hoary head is a crown of glory, if it be found in the way of righteousness. Proverbs 16:31

Train up a child in the way he should go: and when he is old, he will not depart from it. Proverbs 22:6

Investing in Your Marriage

Lay not up for yourselves treasures upon earth, where moth and rust doth corrupt, and where thieves break through and steal: But lay up for yourselves treasures in heaven, where neither moth nor rust doth corrupt, and where thieves do not break through nor steal. Matthew 6:19-20

For where your treasure is, there will your heart be also.
Matthew 6:21

Two are better than one; because they have a good reward for their labour. Ecclesiastes 4:9

A man's heart deviseth his way: but the Lord directeth his steps.
Proverbs 16:9

Investing time, energy, and resources in your marriage pays dividends for a lifetime. - Gary Chapman

Through wisdom is an house builded; and by understanding it is established: And by knowledge shall the chambers be filled with all precious and pleasant riches. Proverbs 24:3-4

She considereth a field, and buyeth it: with the fruit of her hands she planteth a vineyard. Proverbs 31:16

Never Giving Up

And let us not be weary in well doing: for in due season we shall reap, if we faint not. Galatians 6:9

Watch ye, stand fast in the faith, quit you like men, be strong. 1 Corinthians 16:13

For a just man falleth seven times, and riseth up again: but the wicked shall fall into mischief. Proverbs 24:16

Being confident of this very thing, that he which hath begun a good work in you will perform it until the day of Jesus Christ.
 Philippians 1:6

Marriage is a commitment to never give up on each other, even when times are difficult. - Gary Thomas

Therefore, my beloved brethren, be ye stedfast, unmoveable, always abounding in the work of the Lord, forasmuch as ye know that your labour is not in vain in the Lord. 1 Corinthians 15:58

Let us hold fast the profession of our faith without wavering; for he is faithful that promised. Hebrews 10:23

Fighting for Your Marriage

Finally, my brethren, be strong in the Lord, and in the power of his might. Put on the whole armour of God, that ye may be able to stand against the wiles of the devil. Ephesians 6:10-11

Fight the good fight of faith, lay hold on eternal life, whereunto thou art also called, and hast professed a good profession before many witnesses. 1 Timothy 6:12

Submit yourselves therefore to God. Resist the devil, and he will flee from you. James 4:7

For we wrestle not against flesh and blood, but against principalities, against powers, against the rulers of the darkness of this world, against spiritual wickedness in high places. Ephesians 6:12

Fight for your marriage, not against your spouse. The real battle is against forces that would destroy your unity. - Gary Thomas

And they overcame him by the blood of the Lamb, and by the word of their testimony; and they loved not their lives unto the death. Revelation 12:11

The Lord shall fight for you, and ye shall hold your peace. Exodus 14:14

Covenant Keeping

My covenant will I not break, nor alter the thing that is gone out of my lips. Psalms 89:34

When thou vowest a vow unto God, defer not to pay it; for he hath no pleasure in fools: pay that which thou hast vowed. Ecclesiastes 5:4

Yet ye say, Wherefore? Because the Lord hath been witness between thee and the wife of thy youth, against whom thou hast dealt treacherously: yet is she thy companion, and the wife of thy covenant. Malachi 2:14

He hath remembered his covenant for ever, the word which he commanded to a thousand generations. Psalms 105:8

Covenant keeping is the foundation of marriage - a commitment that endures regardless of circumstances. - Gary Thomas

Know therefore that the Lord thy God, he is God, the faithful God, which keepeth covenant and mercy with them that love him and keep his commandments to a thousand generations. Deuteronomy 7:9

If we believe not, yet he abideth faithful: he cannot deny himself. 2 Timothy 2:13

Growing Old Together

The hoary head is a crown of glory, if it be found in the way of righteousness. Proverbs 16:31

Cast me not off in the time of old age; forsake me not when my strength faileth. Psalms 71:9

Even to your old age I am he; and even to hoar hairs will I carry you: I have made, and I will bear; even I will carry, and will deliver you. Isaiah 46:4

They shall still bring forth fruit in old age; they shall be fat and flourishing. Psalms 92:14

Growing old together is a privilege denied to many. Embrace each stage of life as a gift from God. - Billy Graham

The glory of young men is their strength: and the beauty of old men is the grey head. Proverbs 20:29

With the ancient is wisdom; and in length of days understanding. Job 12:12

Leaving a Marriage Legacy

The just man walketh in his integrity: his children are blessed after him. Proverbs 20:7

One generation shall praise thy works to another, and shall declare thy mighty acts. Psalms 145:4

A good man leaveth an inheritance to his children's children: and the wealth of the sinner is laid up for the just. Proverbs 13:22

The memory of the just is blessed: but the name of the wicked shall rot. Proverbs 10:7

Your marriage legacy is not just what you leave behind, but what you live out day by day before those who watch. - Dennis Rainey

And he shall turn the heart of the fathers to the children, and the heart of the children to their fathers, lest I come and smite the earth with a curse. Malachi 4:6

And these words, which I command thee this day, shall be in thine heart: And thou shalt teach them diligently unto thy children, and shalt talk of them when thou sittest in thine house, and when thou walkest by the way, and when thou liest down, and when thou risest up. Deuteronomy 6:6-7

Marriage and Eternity

For in the resurrection they neither marry, nor are given in marriage, but are as the angels of God in heaven. Matthew 22:30

And Jesus answering said unto them, The children of this world marry, and are given in marriage: But they which shall be accounted worthy to obtain that world, and the resurrection from the dead, neither marry, nor are given in marriage. Luke 20:34-35

While we look not at the things which are seen, but at the things which are not seen: for the things which are seen are temporal; but the things which are not seen are eternal. 2 Corinthians 4:18

For we know that if our earthly house of this tabernacle were dissolved, we have a building of God, an house not made with hands, eternal in the heavens. 2 Corinthians 5:1

Marriage is temporal, but the love we learn in marriage prepares us for eternal love with Christ. - Randy Alcorn

Set your affection on things above, not on things on the earth. Colossians 3:2

For our light affliction, which is but for a moment, worketh for us a far more exceeding and eternal weight of glory. 2 Corinthians 4:17

OTHER TOPICAL BIBLES AVAILABLE:

Believer's Topical Bible
Women's Topical Bible
Men's Topical Bible
Teen's Topical Bible
Pastor's Topical Bible
Marriage Topical Bible
Father's Topical Bible
Mother's Topical Bible
Senior's Topical Bible
Minister's Topical Bible

www.ingramcontent.com/pod-product-compliance
Lightning Source LLC
Chambersburg PA
CBHW070614170426
43200CB00012B/2684